GODDESS
SIGNS

ABOUT THE AUTHOR

Angelica Danton has studied and taught in the metaphysical field for over twenty years. She is also a regular radio speaker and broadcaster on New Age topics. She holds a degree in arts from Monash University and a degree in law from the University of Melbourne.

Angelica is a professional astrologer, palmist, tarot reader, and numerologist with an extensive international client base. She comes from a family of intuitives. She is also a regular writer for a number of publications, including the best-selling *Woman's Day* magazine. She is a consultant on many New Age topics for various media groups, and she regularly conducts workshops on the Goddess based on her research. Angelica currently lives in Australia.

GODDESS SIGNS

Which One Are You?

Angelica Danton

2004
Llewellyn Publications
St. Paul, Minnesota 55164-0383, U.S.A.

First Edition
First Printing, 2004

Book design and editing by Joanna Willis
Cover and interior art © 2003 by Svetlana Chmakova
Cover design by Lisa Novak

Library of Congress Cataloging-in-Publication Data
Danton, Angelica, 1965–
    Goddess signs: which one are you? / Angelica Danton.—1st ed.
        p.   cm.
    Includes bibliographical references (p.).
    ISBN 0-7387-0469-5
     1. Goddess religion. I. Title.

    BL473.5.D36 2004
    202'.114—dc22

                                                                    2003066146

Llewellyn Publications
A Division of Llewellyn Worldwide, Ltd.
P.O. Box 64383, Dept. 0-7387-0469-5
St. Paul, MN 55164-0383, U.S.A.
www.llewellyn.com

 Printed in the United States of America on recycled paper

To Bennu,
phoenix and teacher

Contents

PART IV: WARRIOR GODDESS WOMEN

PART V: DARK GODDESS WOMEN

PART VI: GODDESS TYPES & RELATIONSHIPS

Preface

From my research over the last few decades, I became interested in the spiritual empowerment that an understanding of the Chinese signs made possible for both men and women. Then I also began to see how the animal energy of each sign benefitted from being understood on a divine level—that is, from being correlated to the expression of the gods or goddesses from ancient myths and cultures. After all, both the ancient Egyptians and the Aztecs made their gods and goddesses part of their zodiac.

As I continued my personal and professional research, I was amazed by the way an individual's life was so strongly influenced by his or her sign and its divine potential. The divine energy manifests itself in a myriad of forms. By understanding your destiny from your animal sign, you can take a further step toward appreciating your god or goddess potential by using Chinese astrology.

Acknowledgments

There are many divine beings who have contributed to the realization of *Goddess Signs* and the Goddess knows who they are. I have always thought a book is a dream realized in tangible form. It only comes about through gifts of ideas, influences, and visions from many diverse sources (not to mention hard work and application on the part of a number of other individuals!). I feel, therefore, all the people mentioned below had their part to play in the realization of this dream and need to be acknowledged and thanked personally.

Firstly, I would like to thank my family, who have always totally supported my spiritual work and encouraged me to develop my potential. I was fortunate enough to be born into a group of people who had clairvoyance and insight themselves, and who were lovers of literature and words. To my mother, Ellen, thank you for fostering my appreciation of poetry and spirituality. Thanks also to my dad, Ron, who was a secret shaman; my brother Terry, who has always given me the right book at the relevant time; my dear grandfather Les, who dubbed me a "dark horse" (I think he meant Dark Goddess with lots of Sag!); my insightful, musical grandmother Eileen, who taught me to read when I was young; my sister Sharon, who supported me in my college years; my sister Maree, who spent long hours typing up the manuscript, encouraged me, and bought the computer; and my godmother Thelma and my other dear aunt Mabel, who gave me lots of material for understanding the Sun Goddess. I also thank my ancestor Laurence Sterne for the inspiration I have taken from his work.

I would also like to acknowledge the encouragement of many of my friends and associates. Many thanks to (in no particular order) Cath and Rob, who were always there to listen to my issues; Elisabeth Kübler-Ross, who let me read for her and encouraged my career; Helen Ertell, who was a major inspiration for Rat woman and a goddess in her own right; Sharon B. for giving me her insightful vision; Ross and Di for being there and for being wonderful people and friends; Jacquelene for giving me her humor, wit, and support; Craig for letting me borrow his computer in a difficult time; and Bernie for fixing the computer! A special thanks also to Marissa, who met me at the World Prayer Day and was a true soul sister in her loving attitude and generosity. Cheers also to my mate and fellow writer Mark, who suggested I try an American publisher, and my cousins Peter and Chris, who wanted a writer in the family. My thanks also to the late Buddhy Gilbert who, amongst others, gave me the inspiration for the epilogue.

I would also like to thank my educators at college and at school, including my wonderful headmistress Ms. Sampson, who was an independent and original goddess; my English teacher Mr. A. Pyke for including me in the school chronicle and developing my understanding of the English language; and my lecturer at university Professor Barry, who opened the world of American literature to me, including the influences of Thoreau and Whitman. I would also like to acknowledge the excellent English faculty at Monash University, who allowed so many diverse areas to be researched and taught.

Thanks also to my dear animal familiars, both those who wait for me on the other side and those who are with me now. My love and gratitude goes to Panda, Grumps, Trixie, Gem, Milky, Max, Dana, all my pets, and the cheerful blackbirds who live in the front garden. From the animal energy I have learned to understand and appreciate the world of the spirit, and I acknowledge and venerate their sacred gifts to me both as pets and guides.

I should also acknowledge all the wonderful writers and poets who have inspired me to seek my own truths, including the authors J. K. Rowling, Anne Rice, Barbara Walker, Charlotte Brontë, Jane Austen, Virginia Woolf, Scott Cunningham, Silver RavenWolf, Kathleen Burt, Ted Andrews, John Keats, Percy Shelley, and Emily Brontë. They are all divine inspirations in many diverse ways!

I would also like to express my gratitude to my publisher Llewellyn for, firstly, publishing so many wonderful and enlightening books. They have provided me with endless hours of reading on all my favorite topics for so many years. I am honored to be included as one of their authors amongst so many talented, amazing, and magickal people. Thanks personally to Carl Llewellyn Weschcke, who took a chance on my manuscript; my editor, Joanna Willis, for her careful and accurate editing and creative layout; cover designer Lisa Novak and cover artist Svetlana Chmakova for their brilliant artwork, which is a joy to look at; Natalie Harter and Megan Atwood for their help and advice; and my publicist, Beth Scudder.

A special thanks also to Lorrae Willox at *Woman's Day* for encouraging my writing for magazines.

Lastly, thank you to all the wonderful people I have noted in this book, who have inspired me to see the goddess in all.

Introduction

Goddess study is fascinating, diverse, and holds eternal truths. To quote Dion Fortune, one of the original modern female occultists, "All women are Isis" (*Moon Magic*). In studying the diversity of the pantheon of wonderful goddesses who express so much of the complexity and richness of life, I have also used one of the most instructive and greatest keys to inner character devised: Chinese animal astrology.

According to legend, at the conclusion of his life, Buddha called all the animals to him to bid them farewell. Twelve animals came in order, and he assigned a year to each one. From this beginning, the animal zodiac was formed.

Chinese astrology explores a person's character and destiny through an understanding of the animal ruling his or her year of birth. Each animal sign has powerful characteristics and tendencies that affect the destiny of the individual born under its influence. Having studied Chinese astrology for many years, and from the hundreds of case studies I have done in my work as an astrological counselor, I can personally attest to its amazing accuracy.

In the following chapters you will discover your unique energy, both as it manifests in your animal sign, and as it is symbolized in the following Goddess Signs. I have outlined how you can use the magick of your animal sign to reach a greater understanding of yourself and your Goddess Sign, and how your life can be positively enriched by this. (I have written this book primarily for women to explore this aspect, although in chapter 14 the God Signs of men are covered.)

The wonderful secrets of your animal sign can help you to realize your true potential and develop more understanding of your fellow human beings. Your Goddess Sign will give you even deeper knowledge of your spiritual purpose and your karma (or your soul's pathway), while at the same time revealing fascinating insights into your relationships. (The studies and character descriptions in the following chapters can apply equally to homosexual or heterosexual relationships, although I have written the chapters from the latter vantage point. The Goddess Signs for women are the same for both groups, while the relationships dealing with the god and goddess can be transposed to gay relationships as goddess to goddess where appropriate.)

The really liberating part of goddess worship is its amazing variation. As you learn about how the Goddess manifests herself through so many different cultures and races, you are released from the narrow dictates of society with its limiting obsessions of age and status. Shakespeare once wrote of the famed Cleopatra: "Age cannot wither nor custom stale her infinite variety" (*Anthony and Cleopatra*).

I have included names of famous women in the following chapters who share your special Goddess Sign. As you read the descriptions of yourself and your animal sisters, it is important to remember we are all divine and we all have faults. The "jungle" energy may not always seem spiritual, as this depends on what level we take it to. There is a level where the animal becomes divine, and so do we. I have therefore written this book on two major levels: the animal and the goddess.

I have included spellwork for each animal sign incorporating particular magickal symbols, colors, ritual robes, tarot cards, and appropriate incense and herbs. This book is designed for those who want to understand themselves better as well as those who wish to practice specific magickal rituals. An understanding of your Goddess Sign will make your spellcasting much more effective, I have personally found.

In each chapter I have provided information about each associated goddess either because her totem animal matches the animal sign or because specific characteristics match. As a result of reading this book, you may find yourself drawn to deeper research of your favorite goddess identity. You may also create other rituals yourself to suit your personality and needs. Some powerful ritual workshops can be conducted with women of different goddess types working together for particular goals.

THE EXPRESSION OF THE GODDESS IN WOMEN

Goddess energy is present in every woman, though it is expressed in many different ways and forms. We can divide the expression into twelve variations, which are contained in the five goddess types set out below. Each of the variations corresponds to a woman's animal sign as set out in the following chapters. To access goddess energy instinctively, we need to study how the animal sign personalizes the goddess within, and how the different goddess psyches of our sisters will interact with and balance our own energy.

You may have wondered why you have been brought in contact with certain friends and acquaintances. The energies they exude in their aura affect your own in an invisible yet spiritually tangible way. This book will assist you in recognizing the personal traits of your animal sisters and how such interactions affect your life.

To illustrate this point, imagine that your particular energy relates predominantly to the Dark Goddess. This will mean you may have to seek balance from the other goddess types who produce counter energies, such as Sun or Earth Goddess women. You may find yourself surrounded by women born under the sign of the Rooster, who epitomize Sun energy. Being influenced by the Dark Goddess, you may have a tendency toward too much introspection. Perhaps you need to express yourself, and coming into contact with Rooster women will help you stop hiding your light behind a bushel or dwelling on negativity.

To further illustrate the need for inner balance and interactive learning, if you are under the influence of the Moon Goddess, your energy may be one of self-effacement compared to your Sun Goddess sisters. However, Sun Goddess women can be rather ego-centered and may lack the perception of Moon Goddess women. Through interaction, both can learn from the other, or they can choose conflict! The choice is ultimately up to the individual.

Self-knowledge is self-power, which, channeled in the right direction, leads to personal liberation and success. This is what the Age of Aquarius is all about, not just flower power—unless, of course, your sign falls under the goddess Flora!

By studying the animal signs and associated goddesses and incorporating the rituals I have outlined in the following chapters, I'm sure you will develop a greater appreciation of the diversity of spirit surrounding us. Have fun creating your own special personalized magick!

THE GODDESS AND RELATIONSHIPS

Table 1 will help you decipher what type of goddess energy you have according to your Chinese sign. Simply look up your birth date to find your Chinese sign and element, and your corresponding goddess type will be one of five types: Moon, Sun, Earth, Warrior, or Dark Goddess. (There are five main goddess types, but the Snake woman also displays more of the seductive aspects of the Dark Goddess than the others. See page 10.) You may also like to see how I believe the goddess energy is related to your Western astrological sign via Table 2. This will give you an overview of all the influences of the stars and heavens in your chart. Enjoy!

Your animal sign connection to the Goddess is powerful and permeates your relationships to a large degree. You will express these qualities in differing ways according to the goddess energy you were born under. Different goddess energies attract and need different types of mates. Studying your energy in this way will help you learn and understand past relationships and free yourself up for new experiences you may choose to take. This aspect will be studied in chapter 13.

In chapter 14, I discuss briefly the equivalent energies of the god types in men—the god type energy or God Signs—as well as their compatibility with different Goddess Signs.

THE GODDESS TYPES

The Moon Goddess

Goddess energy has traditionally been associated with the powerful lunar cycles and their effects. Women who express the Moon Goddess are intuitive, reflective, and sensitive. They often possess highly feminine characteristics and are deeply mystical.

Moon energy is complex. It ranges from amazing perceptiveness to extreme self-delusion. Women who connect powerfully with their Moon energy are zany and creative. They can be prone to dramatic and sometimes destructive emotions and traumatic life lessons in relationships. They need to develop their inner strength and fortitude.

As the moon is associated with escape, Moon Goddess women need to be wary of addictive substances and escaping from their problems to the dark side of the

Table 1: Chinese Signs, Elements, and Goddess Types by Birthday

MOON GODDESS

Goat		Cat	
Feb 17, 1931-Feb 5, 1932	metal	Feb 2, 1927-Jan 22, 1928	fire
Feb 5, 1943-Jan 24, 1944	water	Feb 19, 1939-Feb 7, 1940	earth
Jan 24, 1955-Feb 11, 1956	wood	Feb 6, 1951-Jan 26, 1952	metal
Feb 9, 1967-Jan 29, 1968	fire	Jan 25, 1963-Feb 12, 1964	water
Jan 28, 1979-Feb 15, 1980	earth	Feb 11, 1975-Jan 30, 1976	wood
Feb 15, 1991-Feb 3, 1992	metal	Jan 29, 1987-Feb 12, 1988	fire

SUN GODDESS

Dragon		Dog	
Jan 23, 1928-Feb 9, 1929	earth	Feb 14, 1934-Feb 3, 1935	wood
Feb 8, 1940-Jan 26, 1941	metal	Feb 2, 1946-Jan 21, 1947	fire
Jan 27, 1952-Feb 13, 1953	water	Feb 18, 1958-Feb 7, 1959	earth
Feb 13, 1964-Feb 1, 1965	wood	Feb 6, 1970-Jan 26, 1971	metal
Jan 31, 1976-Feb 17, 1977	fire	Jan 25, 1982-Feb 12, 1983	water
Feb 17, 1988-Feb 5, 1989	earth	Feb 10, 1994-Jan 30, 1995	wood

EARTH GODDESS

Pig		Rooster		Ox	
Feb 4, 1935-Jan 23, 1936	wood	Jan 26, 1933-Feb 13, 1934	water	Jan 24, 1925-Feb 12, 1926	fire
Jan 22, 1947-Feb 9, 1948	fire	Feb 13, 1945-Feb 1, 1946	wood	Feb 11, 1937-Jan 30, 1938	earth
Feb 8, 1959-Jan 27, 1960	earth	Jan 31, 1957-Feb 17, 1958	fire	Jan 29, 1949-Feb 16, 1950	metal
Jan 27, 1971-Feb 14, 1972	metal	Feb 17, 1969-Feb 5, 1970	earth	Feb 15, 1961-Feb 4, 1962	water
Feb 13, 1983-Feb 1, 1984	water	Feb 5, 1981-Jan 24, 1982	metal	Feb 3, 1973-Jan 22, 1974	wood
Jan 31, 1995-Feb 18, 1996	wood	Jan 23, 1993-Feb 9, 1994	water	Feb 20, 1985-Feb 8, 1986	fire

WARRIOR GODDESS

Horse		Tiger	
Jan 30, 1930-Feb 16, 1931	metal	Feb 13, 1926-Feb 1, 1927	fire
Feb 15, 1942-Feb 4, 1943	water	Jan 31, 1938-Feb 18, 1939	earth
Feb 3, 1954-Jan 23, 1955	wood	Feb 17, 1950-Feb 5, 1951	metal
Jan 21, 1966-Feb 8, 1967	fire	Feb 5, 1962-Jan 24, 1963	water
Feb 7, 1978-Jan 27, 1979	earth	Jan 23, 1974-Feb 10, 1975	wood
Jan 27, 1990-Feb 14, 1991	metal	Feb 9, 1986-Jan 28, 1987	fire

DARK GODDESS

Rat		Monkey		Snake	
Feb 5, 1924-Jan 23, 1925	wood	Feb 6, 1932-Jan 25, 1933	water	Feb 10, 1929-Jan 29, 1930	earth
Jan 24, 1936-Feb 10, 1937	fire	Jan 25, 1944-Feb 12, 1945	wood	Jan 27, 1941-Feb 14, 1942	metal
Feb 10, 1948-Jan 28, 1949	earth	Feb 12, 1956-Jan 30, 1957	fire	Feb 14, 1953-Feb 2, 1954	water
Jan 28, 1960-Feb 14, 1961	metal	Jan 30, 1968-Feb 16, 1969	earth	Feb 2, 1965-Jan 20, 1966	wood
Feb 15, 1972-Feb 2, 1973	water	Feb 16, 1980-Feb 4, 1981	metal	Feb 18, 1977-Feb 6, 1978	fire
Feb 2, 1984-Feb 19, 1985	wood	Feb 4, 1992-Jan 22, 1993	water	Feb 6, 1989-Jan 26, 1990	earth

Table 2: Western Signs and the Goddess Expression

Goddess Sign Energy	Western Astrological Sign	Chinese Animal Sign
Warrior Goddess	Aries: The Ram	Horse
Empress Goddess	Taurus: The Bull	Ox
Sorceress Goddess	Gemini: The Twins	Monkey
Protector Goddess	Cancer: The Crab	Pig
Queen Goddess	Leo: The Lion	Dragon
Enchantress Goddess	Virgo: The Virgin	Cat
Diva Goddess	Libra: The Scales	Rooster
Siren Goddess	Scorpio: The Scorpion	Snake
Huntress Goddess	Sagittarius: The Centaur	Tiger
High Priestess Goddess	Capricorn: The Goat	Dog
Bewitcher Goddess	Aquarius: The Water Bearer	Rat
Nymph Goddess	Pisces: Fish	Goat

moon. The animal signs of the Dog, Cat, and Goat relate to Moon Goddess energy in differing parts of their personalities as outlined in the following chapters.

The following goddesses express the fluctuating energy of the moon and its associated phases, which mirror the cycles of life and its changes.

Examples of Moon Goddesses in Mythology

Diana: Roman goddess of the moon and the woodlands. She is associated with healing, childbirth, and nursing, and was worshipped by the ancient Gauls as well as the Romans.

Selene: Archetypal moon goddess of the Romans.

Famous Moon Goddess Women

Julia Roberts (Goat)   Madonna (Dog)

Nicole Kidman (Goat)   Cher (Dog)

Angelina Jolie (Cat)   Kate Winslet (Cat)

The Sun Goddess

These goddesses are active, charismatic, and life-enhancing. They are ego-centered and proud.

Sun Goddesses desire challenge in life and respect in the public arena. Sun energy creates warm and passionate women who are ambitious and have self-confidence naturally expressing their masculine energies. They enjoy the spotlight and demand high standards from themselves and those around them.

Their greatest challenges are being too status-conscious, taking on too much responsibility, and being insensitive to their power and actions. Sun Goddess women need to watch conceit, anger, and unreasonableness. They often take life at face value without adequate reflection. Yet they have amazing creative ability and are dynamic and versatile. To truly reach their potential, Sun women must practice a little introspection and spiritual development. Without this, their energy will burn up.

The signs of the Dragon and the Rooster express the energy of the Sun Goddess.

Examples of Sun Goddesses in Mythology

Amaterasu: This Japanese goddess is perhaps the most well known of the sun goddesses. In Shinto religion she expresses the affirmation of the life force. She ruled over the universe and possessed immense versatility in the expression of her power. The Japanese people venerated her as one of their most formidable goddesses.

Saule: The great goddess of the sun to the peoples of the Baltic area. She was often shown in a chariot as she spread her warming sun energy to her people.

Famous Sun Goddess Women

Catherine Zeta-Jones (Rooster)   Courtney Love (Dragon)
Britney Spears (Rooster)   Reese Witherspoon (Dragon)
Cate Blanchett (Rooster)   Calista Flockhart (Dragon)

The Earth Goddess

These goddesses are connected with the earth's energy and its nurturing, protective, and healing aspects. Earth women are capable of great achievements in the material world, but are also deeply in need of love, relationships, and family connections.

Devoted and caring, Earth Goddess women are pillars of support in their particular society. Their challenges are overnurturing others and becoming too caught up in the "mother" identity. They need to focus more on the individual self, and stop being influenced by others, as they can easily become a victim. Pig and Ox women relate particularly to the Earth Goddess energy.

Examples of Earth Goddesses in Mythology

Demeter:	The ancient Greek goddess of the earth, corn, and grain, and the mother of the Greek goddess of rebirth, Persephone.
Freya:	Scandinavian earth mother goddess of childbirth, motherhood, and marriage.
Hera:	This Greek goddess symbolized the "victim" mother or wife type, although she was powerful in her own right. Her original name may have been He Era, "The Earth."
Goddess of Malta:	Venerated by the Maltese in over thirty temples, this powerful earth goddess figure dominated Maltese religious thought for centuries.

Famous Earth Goddess Women

Camilla Parker-Bowles (Pig)	Princess Diana (Ox)
Hillary Rodham Clinton (Pig)	Jane Fonda (Ox)
Winona Ryder (Pig)	Enya (Ox)

The Warrior Goddess

Warrior Goddesses are bold, innovative, and energetic. The warrior spirit is forceful and achieving and survives many odds and obstacles.

Warrior Goddess women identify with the discipline and dedication of the soldier and the fighter character. In history, the Warrior Goddesses hold a very important place as inspirers of hope for fighting armies and tribes.

Warrior Goddesses are admirable and awesome but must beware their over-assertiveness and aggression that can alienate them from others. Learning temperance and when to pull their heads in are important lessons for Warrior women, as is balancing their assertiveness with feminine reflection.

Women under the sign of the Horse and Tiger relate well to the Warrior Goddess energy.

Examples of Warrior Goddesses in Mythology

Valkyries: Nordic war-maiden goddesses who rode throughout the world bringing back to the gods the bravest souls who had fallen in battle.

Brigantia: Celtic goddess of battle, regarded as a symbol of victory to the ancient Celts.

Sekhmet: Powerful Egyptian lioness-headed goddess of battle and victory.

Nike: Greek goddess who symbolized victory and success to those in battle. The ancient Romans saw her as Victoria, the goddess of victory over death.

Famous Warrior Goddess Women

Agatha Christie (Tiger)	Barbra Streisand (Horse)
Penélope Cruz (Tiger)	Aretha Franklin (Horse)
Queen Elizabeth II (Tiger)	Cindy Crawford (Horse)

The Dark Goddess

These goddesses are linked to the mysterious and the underworld. They can be complex and magickal, and they have qualities of clairvoyance and shape-shifting (the ability to change persona or soul dynamics to best suit a particular situation). These aspects of themselves will be expressed in their work, relationships, and creativity.

Dark Goddess women are difficult to categorize. Gifted with an extrasensory ability to see through life and its levels, they defy society's norms and conventions and make up their own. Intrigue and interest follow them. Passionate, intense, and often secretive, Dark Goddess women represent the subtle and complex energy of the night.

Women who express the qualities of the Dark Goddess need to beware of self-deception, domination, and dark emotions. They should at all costs avoid dirty politics and power games. The signs of the Rat, Monkey, and the Snake relate particularly well to the energy of the Dark Goddess.

Snake women should also take note that they express another aspect of the Dark Goddess: the Seductive Goddess. These women evoke all that is sensual, seductive, and erotic. The sign of the Snake relates closely to the Seductive Goddess in her erotic energies and capacity to enthrall.

Seductive Goddess women connect their sexuality directly to their power base. Therefore they are very strong women who wield considerable influence over others. Their primary challenges are becoming caught up in their hypnotic power, and losing creativity or succumbing to sensuality. Seductive Goddess women are drawn to power play and politics and often feel the need to be involved with important people. These women have great potential for wisdom and, in their deeper spiritual capacity, healing.

Examples of Dark Goddesses in Mythology

Hecate: Greek queen goddess of magick, the underworld, and the night. She is regarded as one of the most powerful of all the ancient goddesses.

Circe: Greek goddess of sorcery. Circe was a trickster who held dangerous powers.

Persephone: Originally an innocent maiden, the goddess Persephone descended to the underworld and emerged a complex creature with the power to bring the earth the fruits of the hidden.

Lakshmi: Hindu goddess of beauty and sexuality who was the mate of the god Vishnu. She is still invoked by Hindu girls on their wedding day for her power to please her partner.

Aphrodite: Greek goddess of love and power. She was regarded as one of the most significant of Greek goddesses. She was invoked in all manner of love and relationship rituals, spells, and petitions.

Famous Dark Goddess Women

Sarah Jessica Parker (Snake)   Alyssa Milano (Rat)

Audrey Hepburn (Snake)   Cameron Diaz (Rat)

Jennifer Aniston (Monkey)   Kylie Minogue (Monkey)

THE GODDESS POWER OF YOUR ELEMENT

Metal

The element of metal in your year of birth attunes you to the air element and the goddess of the sky, air, and the heavens. Metal-ruled women are intellectual, clever, and analyzing. They love to plan, are careful in execution and get things done efficiently.

Their critical faculties are well developed and they tend to be quite demanding or sometimes unreasonable. Metal energy increases one's capacity to initiate, carry out, and detach. It will assist a female's energy to be more impersonal and/or clinical. Consequently, it can weaken tolerance and femininity.

Metal Goddess women need intelligent, communicative partners.

Mythological Metal Goddess

Saule, Russian sky goddess

Wood

The element of wood in your year of birth attunes you to the goddess of the woods and the forests. Your energy is gentle and sensitive, but you often suffer from insecurity and self-doubt.

Wood-ruled women are psychic, high-strung, and vulnerable. They seek approval and require a creative outlet. Wood Goddess women need a gentle, honest mate who builds their confidence.

Mythological Wood Goddess

Flora, Roman floral goddess

Earth

The element of earth in your birth year attunes you to the power of earth energy. You will be naturally organized, methodical, and nurturing, but can often suffer from being too materialistic, selfish, and narrow-minded.

Earth-ruled women are protective, caring, and grounded, but need to be careful of getting caught in restrictive routines. These women need secure, reliable mates.

Mythological Earth Goddess

Cybele, Anatolian earth goddess

Water

The element of water in your year of birth attunes you to the Water Goddess. Water-ruled women are emotional, instinctive, and inclined to fantasy. They have very powerful mood swings and emotional detachment can be difficult.

Water Goddess women need sympathetic, deeply caring partners with a developed maternal side.

Mythological Water Goddess

Sedna, Inuit sea goddess

Fire

The element of fire in your year of birth attunes you to the Fire Goddess and the energy of fire as an element. You will be a leader, direct and instinctive. However, you may also suffer from insensitivity, bossiness, and an inability to delegate.

Fire-ruled women are passionate, creative, and sexually powerful. They have to be mindful of impatience and greed. Such goddess women need calming and relaxing partners.

Mythological Fire Goddess

Pele, Hawaiian volcano goddess

RITUAL MAGICK AND YOUR GODDESS SIGN

If you are interested in pursuing ritual magick directly linked to your animal sign, there are certain tools that will help to access your psychic energies naturally. I have listed in the beginning of each chapter the colors, incense, herbs, and symbols for each one of the animal signs. Feel open to create rituals of your own using the tools suggested in this book. However, the more knowledge you have of your animal sign, the greater your powers of focus will be, so study the following chapters carefully before attempting the ritual work.

As in ancient Egyptian magick, it is important to link energies between the realm of the divine and the physical dimension. For this reason, possessing a likeness or ornament of your animal sign is helpful. An altar in a sacred area should be created in a private part of your home or garden. This will be your private sanctuary where your meditation and visualization will connect the energy of the goddess with your own free spirit.

For specific invocations, the best practice is to seal your sacred space before and at the end of each ritual. For this purpose, I often invoke the protection of the archangel Michael to oversee my preparations and seal out negative energies. Use the following invocation for the deity or spirit of your choice:

> "[Spirit's name and/or description], seal my space and my aura, allowing only the positive flow of energy in my work."

The further invocation of the Goddess will also help your intentions to be carried out in a positive environment.

It is sometimes difficult for beginners in this area to relate to certain rituals, however, the benefit of animal magick is that it taps into your own energy very quickly. If you are a Cat woman, for example, you will be able to "feel" instinctively the energy of Bastet (the Egyptian cat goddess) or the moon goddesses. Goddess Sign knowledge will make your spellcasting potent in a very personal way. (Note when concluding ritual work with candles to be sure to carefully snuff out the flames.)

NUMEROLOGY AND MEDITATION

To personalize your animal sign further, you can also use numerology to check out how your date of birth affects the expression of your energy and your destiny.

Numerology is the fascinating study of how one's date of birth influences his or her fate. I have often observed how it combines with a person's animal sign in a very unique way. So for your reference, I have added in each animal chapter a list of characteristics based on one's day of birth and animal sign. I am sure you will also enjoy checking out your friends and family to see how accurate this combined reading is. You can also view the number as your lucky number or your day number.

To calculate your number using numerology, reduce your date of birth to a single digit (if it is not already one) by adding the numbers together. For example, if you were born on the twenty-ninth day of the month, your number is 2 (29 = 2 + 9 = 11, 1 + 1 = 2). If you were born on the fourteenth day of the month, you number is 5.

In each chapter, I have also included meditations and rituals for accessing your inner goddess by working with your personal animal energy and your Goddess Sign. The benefit of meditating on the goddess is that you will begin to feel more at one with her, allowing her to manifest special insights and inspirations in your life. Meditation of this type is guided in that you are given certain images or rituals of the goddess to work with. As already mentioned, the kinds of meditation suggested are not exhaustive, and you may of course create many more of your own once you have familiarized yourself with the attributes of your Goddess Sign. Always meditate in a quiet, tranquil space without interruptions.

You may also like to bring the goddess energy into your life by naming a favorite pet after her or hanging her image in your home. She loves to be honored, remembered, and invoked, so now that you know what your sign is, you can invite her in in a way you never dreamed of! Above all, have fun with your Goddess Sign and celebrate your divinity!

PART I

Moon Goddess Women

Goat Woman
THE NATURAL NYMPH

CHARMS AND SYMBOLS

Tarot card:	The Moon, which represents the emotions
Moon phase:	Waxing
Celestial bodies:	Neptune, the moon
Herbs and plants:	Aloe, camellia
Colors:	Whites, creams, greens
Crystals and gemstones:	Moonstone, clear quartz
Incense:	Lemon balm, sandalwood, gardenia
Lucky day:	Monday
Lucky numbers:	2, 7, 11, 20
Ritual colors:	Whites, blues, silver
Ritual robes:	Cotton, chiffon, light fabrics
Magickal symbols:	Mermaids, shells, fish, keys
Goddesses:	The moon, the maiden, the virginal, the feminine
Theme song:	"(What a) Wonderful World" by Louis Armstrong

ASSOCIATED GODDESSES FOR THE GOAT WOMAN

Flora: Roman goddess of vegetation and fertility who was also the original nymph. She is usually portrayed surrounded by fresh flowers.

Sedna: North American goddess of water and the sea. Once a beautiful maiden, she became the ruler of the oceans. She guards the waters and is honored by fishermen.

Oxun: African goddess of the water in all forms. She is usually depicted beautifully adorned as a stunning young woman sitting at the foot of a waterfall. She was regarded as a patron deity and goddess of beauty and femininity. She also held court over mediumship and hidden knowledge.

Freya: Scandinavian goddess of beauty. She often took the form of a she-goat to cavort on earth.

POSITIVE TRAITS

natural	fresh
feminine	diplomatic
unaffected	caring
sensitive	idealistic
ethereal	nurturing
thoughtful	spiritual
gentle	creative
passionate	perceptive
refined	intelligent
discerning	loving

NEGATIVE TRAITS

unsophisticated	passive
insecure	touchy
ungrounded	manipulative
vacillating	naive
acquiring	calculating
unrealistic	fussy
impractical	critical
finicky	overanalytical
detached	cold
weak	indifferent

fAMOUS GOAT WOMEN

Julia Roberts · Nicole Kidman · Barbara Stanwyck · Jane Austen
Evita Perón · Whoopi Goldberg · Catherine Deneuve · Kate Hudson
Katharine Hepburn · Jennifer Love Hewitt · Pamela Anderson · Laura Dern
Mira Sorvino · Judy Davis · Veronica Lake · Simone de Beauvoir
Christina Ricci · Heather Mills

GOAT WOMAN'S NUMBER

1 Sprightly and vivacious, you like to take the lead and be noticed. Try acting!

2 Docile and refined, you love to empathize with others. A marvelous counselor.

3 You can make a wonderful creative writer or thinker. You need to teach others.

4 You may need to build a castle, but not in the sky! There is a determined streak in you that inspires others.

5 Personality and natural style are yours. You work best in a busy but free environment.

6 You have the Earth Mother strongly represented in you. You need the security of family.

7 You are a highly sensitive, insightful Goat. Use your discernment and travel overseas.

8 Natural resilience and toughness balance your other Goat qualities. You can help to reform life for others.

9 Visionary Goat! You like to look at the big picture.

THE NYMPH!

The Goat woman is an exquisitely feminine creature in the classic romantic mode. No matter what her age, her goddess energy is forever linked to the fragile, emerging maiden full of wonder and promise. In this sense, she emulates both the moon goddesses and the nymphs of legend. Yet the goat in myth and legend has been associated with the god Pan and is one of the major symbolic animals of the earth's energy in its positive and negative aspects.

The Goat woman carries herself with refinement and dignity and creates an almost otherworldly aura about her. Although she is distinctively gentle to the point of fragility in appearance, she shows strength and valor in her undertakings. Her sensitivity makes her a fabulous creative artist or entertainer.

The current twenty-first-century confusion over male and female roles and what part each should play has assisted the rise of ultrafeminine Goat women artists like Julia Roberts and Nicole Kidman. These Goat leading ladies stir up memories of feisty maidens of old and create a romantic link to the past while demonstrating the Moon Goddess's evocative emotions. Nicole Kidman's portrayal of a fragile yet determined woman in *Moulin Rouge* artfully illustrates the Goat woman's powerful yet elusive femininity, while Julia Roberts dazzles us with her on-screen versatility and womanly charm.

Literate, clever, refined, and perceptive, the Goat woman sees deeply into the heart of the matter and comes up with some incredible insights. Take a look at the feminine wisdom shown in almost every Jane Austen novel and you will appreciate the understanding the Goat woman has of the feminine psyche. (You will also appreciate her romantic concept of heroes!)

The Goat woman often seeks a life of peace, surrounding herself with loved ones in an idyllic country setting like Austen's novels. The reality for her, however, is probably a hectic and busy lifestyle that leaves her longing for serenity.

A Goat woman can be hypersensitive and is one of the touchiest, most delicate of the animal signs. Her tendency to become dependent on her loved ones and those close to her should be tempered with a development of her creativity.

The Goat woman, despite her talents, often suffers painful periods of low self-esteem. Those close to her should help her balance these times carefully before they overwhelm her.

The younger Goat woman tends to operate on a very emotional level. This tendency may cause her to become very dependent in an unproductive relationship or obsessed with a failed passion. There is, deep inside her, a desire to believe passionately in the romantic hero concept, and to fantasize that any man she is interested in will fulfill and complete her life. This can lead to sharp disappointments when reality is revealed, and it may be difficult for her to accept human nature.

Although her appearance is ultrafeminine and her manner gentle and reflective, the Goat woman is capable of quite a good deal of manipulation and planning. She is formidably ambitious. She has very powerful desires and passions firing just below her feminine surfaces and she can be determined to achieve her desires regardless of the consequences. She can be physically driven and often possesses a strong sexual drive.

She generally prefers classically handsome and dashing mates, and usually has a number of dalliances in her life. If she does settle down, it will happen more by accident than purposeful design.

The Goat woman's nurturing energy causes her to collect strays and attracts mates with a desire to be looked after. These mates, seeking motherly comfort, will often carry emotional baggage into the relationship. The Goat woman often takes on a healing role in such relationships, only to discover the issues are too deep for someone as close as a mate to solve.

It is important for a Goat woman to avoid situations where she is manipulated or controlled by an overly possessive partner. Her strong link with the powerful emotional element of water makes her susceptible to codependency. She also needs to develop emotional detachment and remove her rose-colored glasses long enough to allow her intuition to come to the fore. Like her other Moon Goddess sisters, she must learn to be herself and not mirror only the desires of her partner.

An important part of a Goat woman's development is the realization of who she really is. If she begins to appreciate the goddess energy within her, she will realize that we are here to fulfill ourselves. Partnership is a wonderful thing, but it is not all life has to offer. We are mainly here to learn, and the best study environment is often where we are not distracted.

In many cases, the Goat woman's karma or fate is to experience a series of difficult relationships before she finds her real soul mate. Yet her romantic nature refuses to accept defeat. Goat woman Katharine Hepburn loved her partner Spencer Tracy passionately through many difficulties but retained her own life and artistry.

It is vital for the Goat woman to ground herself in life by developing her potential and her practical sides. She must avoid escaping into fantasy too often. In this way she will find true fulfillment and become a wonderful force!

GOAT WOMAN AND LOVE

The powerful depths of the Goat woman's emotions link her symbolically with the element of water. Water has long been seen as an expression of the emotions in dreams and visions. In ancient Greek legend, the water nymph was a feminine creature who could not survive without the water around her. Likewise, the Goat woman needs to be emotionally sustained if she is to be fulfilled.

The water nymph was said to have the power to heal, prophesy, and inspire. The Goat woman, too, may find this power within herself. She can, therefore, learn of the potential of her innermost feelings and their effect on others by associating them with the power of water. She essentially represents a nurturing and delicate energy to a mate, and unless she really understands her deeper self, she will never find what she needs.

When a mate becomes attracted to a Goat woman, there is always an attraction to the healing and nurturing she possesses. However, unless the Goat woman learns to detach from her partner at the appropriate times, she may frighten her spouse with the power of the sea she contains within her. The partner may experience psychological "drowning" in the Goat woman's depths. The darkness of the sea is hypnotic, but it can also be overwhelming if there is too much of it surrounding us.

Many Goat women clients complain of their lovers' request for space and cannot understand why a relationship that has been very close suddenly becomes distant. Goat women need to find the balance between their nurturing side and their creativity.

Often a career in a human growth area will help a Goat woman truly find herself. In this type of work she will be able to spread out the power of her energies

Goat Woman and Compatibility

Goat & Rat
♡

Difficult. Rat is a bit frenetic for Goat's quieter pace. Goat will fret and Rat will get bored with the pace.

Goat & Ox
♡♡

Stability is an important issue for both, so it could be a powerful match. The Ox does not mind providing the companionship Goat requires.

Goat & Tiger
♡

This one will only succeed where Tiger can overlook the touchiness of the Goat. Both seem to have lots of feeling, but there is also danger of arguments and misunderstandings.

Goat & Cat
♡♡♡

Good mix of energies. These two have the capacity to create peace together. Cat has a sense of taste and art that is close to the Goat's.

Goat & Dragon
♡

Can work, but the Dragon's large personality may overpower Goat.

Goat & Snake
♡♡

This union can have the right touch, as both love gentle moments and their privacy. But Goat will sometimes be hurt by the secretiveness of the Snake mate.

Goat & Horse
♡♡♡

These two are kindred spirits and the empathy will be powerful. They appreciate each other's sense of freedom.

Goat & Goat
♡♡♡♡

Very good team. Both of them value the benefits of peaceful living and family values. They need to watch excessive escapism though.

Goat & Monkey
♡

The Goat will be fascinated with Monkey, but the union will have major problems. They both suffer from overenthusiasm and will hesitate on who will take the lead at times.

Goat & Rooster
♡♡

Can work if the Goat takes second place. The Rooster loves to be cock of the walk, and will give the Goat a few challenges.

Goat & Dog
♡♡♡

Good. Goat is content and happy with this most loyal sign. Goat helps Dog to deal with dark moods, but they must be very careful to be moderate in their lives.

Goat & Pig
♡♡♡

A solid, no-nonsense team. The Pig is jovial and kind, which Goat adores.

♡♡♡♡ = excellent   ♡♡♡ = good   ♡♡ = fair   ♡ = difficult

and not just focus on personal bonds, which may otherwise suffer from too much intensity.

The Goat woman may fall victim to depression and withdrawal in times of personal disappointment, and should foster a close network of loving friends to help her get over any temporary downturns in life. She will also be placed in situations where she will be faced with challenging circumstances that will teach her to develop independence and courage.

The correct partner for a Goat woman is someone with a mature personality who appreciates her feminine freshness and dynamism without feeling personally threatened by it. The paradox for the Goat woman is that the right partner for her is often a person who is not interested in being nurtured so much as being the one to nurture her!

The classic fairy tale "The Little Mermaid" has relevance for the Goat woman in its portrayal of a lovely mermaid yearning for the affections of the unattainable prince. The mermaid tragically loses herself in her emotions. Changing her true self does not lead to the person of her dreams.

For the Goat woman, the maturing process of her emotions may be painful, but she has the power to become wise and contribute much to the world if she looks within and finds her own power. She will always retain her unaffected natural self.

As a wife and mother, she is a natural and is very interested in her children. Normally they will appreciate her gentle and nurturing energy. She must beware of being too indulgent with them however!

GOAT WOMAN AND HEALTH

A Goat woman can suffer from reversals in health during her life, as she is not always the most robust of the signs. She needs to practice common sense in this area of life and remember to look after her body. Sensitive points are her bones, skeletal system, stomach, and gynecological system. Her emotions can affect her health badly, and she needs to be aware of mental depression and mood swings. A healthy diet is very beneficial for her, as is yoga and regular relaxation. She would benefit from regular breaks taking in nature at the beach or in a forest.

GOAT WOMAN AND FINANCES

The Goat woman may have a rather casual attitude toward finances and sometimes lose money through carelessness. A sensible financial plan is very important and she needs to think of her future security. She loves little extravagances and spends quite freely. However, she often has rather good luck in this area and can usually manage quite well.

Real estate is a good investment for the Goat woman, as is solid stocks or bonds.

GOAT WOMAN AS A CHILD

As a child, the Goat woman is ethereal and classically fairylike. She will be drawn to romantic, creative pursuits and enjoy theatre and dance lessons, acting, and mime. She will have a very active fantasy life and enjoy any aspect of life that helps her dream.

She will be an incredibly sensitive youth easily affected by her parents' own energy and relationship. She will react to the family unit acutely, and any variations in personal security will affect her deeply. The Goat child requires plenty of careful and unobtrusive nurturing, and will benefit from a family environment that instills commonsense routines to help ground her fertile imagination.

In adolescence, some dramas can be expected in the realm of the emotions. A firm grounding in other areas will assist her to cope better through this intense roller-coaster period.

GOAT WOMAN AND CAREER

Her nurturing and perceptive abilities make the Goat woman a superb healer, counselor, or therapist. She would also make an excellent caregiver as she loves to have a career that brings out this side of her personality. Suitable choices for her include childcare worker, teacher, or psychologist. She could also excel as a creative artist if disciplined enough, as her powerful and deep emotions provide her with excellent focus and ability to capture the imagination.

Unsuitable careers are anything involving cutthroat competition or the need to undermine others to gain promotion. The Goat woman's gentle nature would not fare well in the type of professions that require such tactics.

GOAT WOMAN IN THE TWENTY-FIRST CENTURY

The Goat woman's feminine character and her capacity to exude security to others are valued traits of the twenty-first century. Goat women will find themselves valued members in this society, especially in either the arts or as community volunteers. The Goat woman may also find her talents needed in local politics. She has the type of honest, approachable, personal charisma that would do well in public office.

GOAT WOMAN AND SPIRITUALITY

The Goat woman naturally relates to the power of the otherworld. I have named her "the nymph" because once she taps into her true goddess, she possesses the ability to bring the otherworld's energy closer to this one.

For ritual work invoking the Goddess, the Goat woman should have a place as close as possible to nature. If she lives in an apartment, then she should create a natural sanctuary in her living area by surrounding herself with indoor plants and pictures of calming rivers or forests. If given permission, she may even like to paint her own mural on the wall on which to meditate.

RITUAL WORK FOR THE GOAT WOMAN

INVOKING SEDNA FOR SPECIAL REQUESTS

Ritual Tools

· White and gold candles
· Water in a clear bowl
· Lemon balm incense
· Citrine quartz crystal
· Small pieces of parchment
· A piece of silk material or garment
· A shell or a picture of a mermaid

Ritual Time

Just after the new moon period.

Create an altar with the above tools. Light the candles and incense. Concentrate on the power of the feminine in its pure, virginal state. Write on the parchment any requests and use a new piece for each request. Take a little time to meditate on each one separately.

Invoke the goddess Sedna as follows:

> "Great goddess Sedna, I call upon your power and purity to assist me in my everyday life. I realize the divine power of your femininity within me and ask you to enable me to bring it forth. As you are both virtuous and wise, I invoke your power to enhance my natural sensitivities and to strengthen my resolve. I petition you for the realization of my desires as follows: [*state your petitions*]."

Fold the pieces of parchment into the silk cloth and sprinkle the water over them. Snuff out the candles and devote your request to the power of Sedna. Leave the parchment on your altar space for seven days and as your desires are fulfilled, thank the goddess.

INVOKING FLORA FOR LOVE

Ritual Tools
· Fresh-cut flowers of any kind
· Rose quartz
· One cup uncooked rice
· One red candle

Ritual Time
Waxing moon and, if possible, when in Taurus or Libra.

Spend some time out in the moonlight gathering flowers for the ceremony. Create your altar, light the candles, and invoke the goddess as follows:

> "Flora, goddess of the flowers, I honor your origin as a nymph. In the same way I seek to blossom and flower in my favorite energy and to nurture those around me in a gentle way. I petition you for love to enter my life."

Throw the petals of the flowers over the altar space and think of the beauty and power of Flora. Then cover the altar with the rice, considering the blessings of the goddess and the rice's fertility association.

Conclude the ritual by dedicating your rose quartz to the goddess and snuffing out the candle. Leave the quartz in the moonlight to absorb its energy for as long as you wish, then keep it somewhere close to where you sleep.

MEDITATION FOR CALM AND DE-STRESSING

Relax somewhere comfortable and visualize yourself walking on a winding foot-path through a forest. You come to a clearing and there in front of you is a magnificent waterfall. It flows from a high hill down along a steep gully to a deep, secluded water hole. You watch the water run down this fall with a gentle focus to meet the pool's water below. You can hear birds singing and the sound of the waterfall running over the rocks and splashing to the pool below.

Imagine yourself removing all your clothes, from your jacket and top to your shoes. Remove everything, even your jewelry.

You are now standing naked in front of this pool and there is no one but you and nature. You are perfectly safe. You have no fear. Your higher self is in this place with you and you have no anxiety or worry.

You are now diving into the water hole. As you do, release all your stress to the water. Swim over to the fall until you are under it and feel the gentle drops of mist against your face. Now think of whatever is causing you pain or worry and let the fresh, clean waterfall wash all your anxieties away.

Stay in your pool for however long it takes to wash away your anxiety. Visit it each time you need to replenish your soul. It will always be there for you, and the best part is, no one else knows how to reach it but you!

Dog Woman
THE NATURAL HIGH PRIESTESS

CHARMS AND SYMBOLS

Tarot card:	The High Priestess, which represents detachment and wisdom
Moon phase:	Waning to new moon
Celestial bodies:	The moon, Earth
Herbs and plants:	Irish moss, gardenia, lemon balm, moonwort
Colors:	Black, white
Crystals and gemstones:	Moonstone, pearl
Incense:	Myrrh, jasmine, sandalwood
Lucky day:	Monday
Lucky numbers:	15, 24
Ritual colors:	Black, white, red
Ritual robes:	Velvets, pure linen, hemp, raw silk
Magickal symbols:	Dogs, circles, hearts, home
Goddesses:	The guardians, the wise ones, the moon goddesses
Theme song:	"I Love My Dog" by Cat Stevens

ASSOCIATED GODDESSES FOR THE DOG WOMAN

Sarama: Indian goddess of domesticated animals. Her sacred animal was the dog.

Themis: Greek goddess of justice and order. She was portrayed holding scales and the sword.

Ixtab: Savior goddess of the ancient Mayan people. She rescued the spirits of those who ended their lives through suicide.

Selket: Egyptian goddess of protection often depicted with a scorpion on her head. She was associated with healers and shamans, and in the Egyptian culture she was believed to give help in their work and protection from poison.

POSITIVE TRAITS

helpful	nostalgic
nonthreatening	caring
passionate	gentle
committed	discreet
driven	deep
trusting	loyal
artistic	disciplined
principled	idealistic
protective	sensitive
reserved	unassuming
honorable	nonjudgmental

NEGATIVE TRAITS

martyr complex	emotional
overprotective	smothering
obsessive	extreme
workaholic	naive
critical	narrow-minded
lives in past	shy
moody	self-centered
self-destructive	secretive
withdrawn	passive
impractical	suspicious
dependent	rigid

FAMOUS DOG WOMEN

Dolly Parton · Susan Sarandon · Sally Field · Shirley MacLaine
Michelle Pfeiffer · Jennifer Lopez · Mariah Carey · Naomi Campbell
Ella Wheeler Wilcox · Liza Minnelli · Uma Thurman · Laura Bush
Jennifer Connelly · Judy Garland · Sophia Loren · Ava Gardner
Cher · Lara Flynn Boyle · Judi Dench · Madonna

DOG WOMAN'S NUMBER

1 Bossy and well-meaning, you seem to be the shoulder everyone leans on, Ms. Dog warrior!

2 A caring, easy-going Dog, you practice a fair bit of humility. Watch deception.

3 You talk more than the average Dog and like to be spoilt. You need plenty of challenges.

4 Grounded Dog. You often protect those around you and need no reminder of your duty. Be careful of extreme behavior.

5 You are witty and like to experience new places and people. You love to travel and make an excellent companion to a fellow explorer!

6 Family means everything. You will fuss over your pack with deep emotions and creativity.

7 You have a strong nose for sniffing out trouble and can be an excellent policewoman or investigator. You will counsel all those around you and offer up advice wisely!

8 Can be a very powerful Dog! Watch those strong beliefs though, as there could be a streak of obsessional tendencies here. Learn to relax and contemplate the ideas of others too. Mixed views will bring you great insight.

9 A leading-light Ms. Dog. You should be in politics, or at least a place where your actions will make a difference.

THE HIGH PRIESTESS!

The Dog woman is the guardian, the gatekeeper. In ancient myth, the dog has always been associated with protection and assigned the responsibility of keeping the balance between the upper and lower worlds.

I have named the Dog woman the "high priestess" because she carries within her the wisdom of the priestess. In a spiritual sense, she can develop this part of herself. She contains in her a great well of power, although she expresses it in a quiet and unassuming way.

Just like the animal that is her totem, the Dog woman seeks always to protect and cherish those close to her. She considers them her pack and thinks in terms of collective concerns, not just her own. She is naturally seen as an integral part of any working team, and is the rock in her family group. She is loyal, faithful, and patient, and seeks to provide stable ground for and to protect her loved ones—at times even at great cost to her.

In the major arcana card of the Fool in the tarot, the dog is depicted as supporting and protecting the Fool as he is about to step to his death from a cliff. The grounding energy of the dog warns the Fool of his danger.

The Dog woman is a doer more than a talker, and drawn to achieve on a higher level. Her natural reliability, powerful drive, and deep emotional personality make her a highly precious individual. She is capable of tremendous achievements as she has great endurance and staying power. She can be extremely committed to any cause she takes on and will fight for equality. She will feel for those less fortunate than herself and will truly root for the underdog.

Dog lady Shirley MacLaine brings her Dog woman zeal to everything in her life: acting, dancing, writing, and personal spirituality. Lara Flynn Boyle portrays a serious lawyer in the television series *Law and Order*—typical of the Dog woman's steely determination. Judy Garland's portrayal of Dorothy in the *Wizard of Oz* epitomizes another side of the Dog's persona: that of a wonderful, caring companion who befriends the lonely and lost.

The Dog lady is normally a direct and loyal individual. Other human beings, however, do not always have the same ethics as her and she may suffer some tough lessons in this regard. Although she is slow to give herself as a lover or friend, paradoxically, once she does, she can be far too idealistic about her relationships. She does not always pick up on deceptive behavior in others, and she lacks some of the discretion of the other signs, especially when emotionally involved.

There is a deep seriousness about the Dog lady's personality. Her emotions are very strong and her feelings are intense and prevailing. Any tendency to become too withdrawn or depressed needs to be watched carefully, and the Dog lady should endeavor to lift herself out of these episodes of emotional lows. Like her sisters under the Snake sign, the Dog woman must also restrain tendencies to alleviate pain through inappropriate ways such as substance abuse. As the Dog lady is naturally disciplined, this seems peculiar to her psychic makeup, but she can be subject to serious bouts of sadness and depression, which she may find overwhelming.

Unless the Dog woman learns to handle her volatile emotions, she can become very affected by them. A disappointment in love, the loss of a loved one, or sudden reversals in fate can devastate her. This can be attributed largely to her helping nature and the part of her that likes to see everything in an ideal way. She often strains herself beyond her limits in the pursuit of getting it right until it proves overburdening.

The Dog woman needs a powerful support network around her. Her intimates are usually only her closest family circles and a few close friends, but for these individuals, she will do anything!

To understand the Dog woman's emotional energy you need only to compare it to the nature of a dog. It is difficult to win its trust, but once you do, you have a friend for life. It does not give up on you, even if mistreated!

The Dog woman seeks security and reliability in her relationships. She has a tendency to become the savior for those she loves, and sometimes she plays the role too well. As she matures spiritually and emotionally, she begins to develop emotional detachment and will respect her own needs more.

DOG WOMAN AND LOVE

The Dog woman loves seriously and with dedication. It is difficult for her to let go of an ideal or dream in love as she longs passionately to nurture and cherish. This makes her an ideal mate; she is patient, caring, and usually very committed once she gets over her initial reserve. However, the Dog woman has to be appreciated in return, otherwise she will be very sad.

She is capable of immense acts of devotion, but unfortunately this leaves her open to severe episodes of unrequited love. She will devote care and attention to parties to no avail. She has a tendency to make huge sacrifices for a loved one, only to be deeply disappointed for the lack of love in return. The Dog woman needs a similarly devoted family-minded mate to keep her happy.

Despite her many sterling characteristics and qualities, the Dog lady is often in need of a partner to lighten her up and provide a touch of humor and tolerance to her often-heavy life. She requires nurturing and help through her difficult periods. Her powerful emotions can lead to certain darker expressions, especially with a difficult or manipulative mate. She needs to avoid extremes of mood, temper, and jealousy, as these negative self-destructive tendencies can overwhelm her. Unfortunately, the Dog woman may put up with abusive and difficult mates. She must be careful in her selection, and remember the energy of the sign she is born under.

I have noticed that Dog women often see themselves in the role of the savior. This is an extension of their desire to protect, and although they mean the best for their partners, Dog women must not let their desires cloud the true picture.

The Dog woman's propensity to live in the past can hold her back—literally. She finds divorce and endings very painful and can suffer from great loneliness after a failed affair. In these times she needs to quickly swing back into an active and balanced life or she will become reclusive and remorseful. A development of her spiritual side expressed in acts like caring for others or doing community work will give the Dog woman the channel she needs in such depressive states. She will bounce back once she begins to feel useful and appreciated again. The Dog woman is one sign that does need people around her to help her get over down periods. If her family life is happy, she will innately turn her energy toward caring for others.

As a wife, the Dog woman is loyal and supportive but hypersensitive. She fulfills herself as a mother, as she deeply cherishes her pups. Yet, again in this area, she should take care of her emotional health and not get too upset with family ups and downs. She sometimes takes the welfare of her offspring too seriously and lacks the ability to detach from them.

Dog Woman and Compatibility

Dog & Rat
♡♡♡

A solid couple as both can learn to trust each other. There is natural empathy and true love can grow.

Dog & Ox
♡♡♡

Good mutual respect is here and a loyal association seems set for both. Trust is natural between two such straightforward signs.

Dog & Tiger
♡♡

Tiger is very changeable and this will unnerve solid Dog. But if Tiger learns to trust Dog's sometimes-secretive side, they can be best mates.

Dog & Cat
♡

These two signs can attract each other, but are polar opposites in many ways! Though they value sensitivity and privacy, the Dog has no time for the games Cat likes to play! Difficult union likely.

Dog & Dragon
♡

Opposites. Dragon is protective too, but will domineer too much for Dog's fair-play personality. The Dragon will not easily give Dog the authority it needs either.

Dog & Snake
♡♡

Can be quite a successful team if Snake is honest. Snake likes Dog's deeper side.

Dog & Horse
♡♡

Can be positive if the Horse learns to give back. Dog favors Horse in many ways and will be honest in love.

Dog & Goat
♡♡♡

Goat can be a bit lazy for Dog's hard work ethic. But if they find mutual endeavors, they make good solid companions.

Dog & Monkey
♡♡♡

Monkey will keep Dog guessing and too many tricks may unsettle Dog's need for stability. However, if Monkey is ready to settle down, they can make a very suitable couple.

Dog & Rooster
♡♡♡

A good team. Both have common philosophies and will stand by one another in tough times. The Rooster can find a way to cheer Dog up.

Dog & Dog
♡♡♡♡

These two Canines love sincerely and will keep their pack well together. Their family values and ethics match beautifully, though both need to watch moods.

Dog & Pig
♡♡♡♡

Good news as Pig admires the steadiness of Dog's character, and they should share a strong sense of humor that will keep them together through thick and thin.

♡♡♡♡ = excellent   ♡♡♡ = good   ♡♡ = fair   ♡ = difficult

DOG WOMAN AND HEALTH

The Dog lady's health is normally quite strong. However, she is susceptible to the occasional bout of depression and illness caused more often than not by her strongly emotional nature. Her emotional side can eat away at her usual robust vitality and she can suffer from nervous upsets, stress, and anxiety.

The Dog woman needs to be less serious in her outlook on life and its associated dramas and problems. She should also exercise a little more detachment in her personal sphere, as she tends to feel for the underdog and will adopt others' problems. Though an admirable quality, this can leave her open to more stress than she should be trying to cope with.

The Dog lady should also eat well and sleep more, as this helps replenish her tension-prone nervous system. She should also avoid overindulgence in alcohol or other substances, as she has a personality that is very unsuitable for either in excess. She cannot take the mental and emotional upheaval that results from abuse in these areas.

DOG WOMAN AND FINANCES

The Dog lady's sense of preparing for that rainy day is linked to her Moon Goddess archetype. Like the dog that buries her bone for later, so does the Dog lady protect her future life.

The Dog woman is normally an excellent saver and will attempt to acquire property or other serious assets by a certain age. She is not generally a greedy or overmaterialistic person, but one who wants the comforts of home secured for her later retirement. She normally attains this goal.

Her major challenge in this area will be the tendency to give her money away to those she feels she needs to help. The Dog lady need not curb her generous nature, which is such an endearing part of her personality, but should watch she's not left out in the cold from being too generous!

DOG WOMAN AS A CHILD

Ms. Dog is a rather serious puppy compared to her other sister animal signs. She is very thoughtful, and at times pensive, but loves to discover things!

Although the Dog child will exhibit characteristics of hypersensitivity and gentleness, she will also display a steady determination and a powerful will to succeed. Like a dog with a bone (as the saying goes), she will get a hold on something and endeavor to complete it, whether that is a chore, a game, or a topic of conversation!

Usually the female Dog child is easy to handle and well behaved. She will take everything you say to heart, so discipline must be used with her sensitivity in mind. The major challenge is likely to be her stubbornness or tendency to secrecy.

Dog children need privacy in their lives, and will appreciate a room of their own at an early age. They love to look after smaller or younger children, and enjoy being given a reasonable amount of responsibility. Dog children have a charming but intense expression and beautiful eyes.

As an adolescent, the Dog lady is likely to have mood swings. She can also be very conscious of peer pressure; wanting to fit in to a certain degree may cause her undue pain. She is a good leader and enjoys responsibility. She usually matures fairly quickly, and will forego teenage pressures to conform.

DOG WOMAN AND CAREER

The Dog woman is a natural achiever and will excel in any career that gives her room to develop and test her ideals. She is often drawn to areas of justice, and her natural empathetic nature and strong sense of fairness may also lead her to politics and social welfare. She would also shine brilliantly as a manager or initiator among people. She loves to fight for a good cause, and is attracted to careers in law enforcement. As an artist she is tremendously determined and gifted, and is likely to be talented in more than one area.

The worst careers for the Dog lady include manual labor and administrative work or office-type careers, as she needs to feel fire in her job and a sense of challenge and purpose.

Possible careers to suit the Dog lady include policewoman, politician, civil rights activist, social worker, artist, writer, technical expert, or researcher. Given her methodical nature, she will excel in jobs that require persistent and moral courage. As an artist, she will usually combine this talent with a private spiritual purpose or goal, as she will not generally be satisfied with public accolades or large monetary rewards alone. The Dog lady needs to feel she has accomplished something for the good of society.

DOG WOMAN IN THE TWENTY-FIRST CENTURY

The Dog woman does not mind hard work, and will be well equipped to take on the challenges of the new century. She has a commanding force to succeed in her endeavors, and in a period of rapidly changing social values, she will no doubt shine as a reformer and leader.

The Dog woman may, at first, find stepping into the traditionally male-dominated careers confusing, but once she accepts her role, she will move mountains with her special dedication and idealism. She should become involved in these areas, as her potential to initiate new social awareness will be immensely valuable. Her kind spirit will permeate areas that need a breath of fresh air.

DOG WOMAN AND SPIRITUALITY

The Dog woman's spirituality often causes her to suffer, and she needs to develop her inner spiritual muscle to cope with this. She cares deeply about the world, and focuses on issues that she knows will ultimately affect herself and those around her. She has instinctual knowledge of the darker side of the emotions and how they can play a part in human suffering and outcomes.

One of the Dog woman's main challenges is to surmount her extremely powerful feelings. She has the capacity to gain much from a study of her spiritual self, as it gives her the extra balance she needs.

Intense Dog lady Shirley MacLaine has matured into a detached High Priestess who views her entire life as a progression of spirit. She should stand as an inspiration to all sister Dogs to delve into their own spiritual wells and pull themselves free of the physical and somewhat insignificant concerns of the material world. Her insights will strengthen and protect her.

The Dog woman relates to the goddess Themis in her ability to make a stand. She believes in fighting for the underdog, and her innate sense of justice will always help her in this pursuit. She also relates to the Moon Goddess in the sensitive feelings she has (like a dog that bays at the moon).

RITUAL WORK fOR THE DOG WOMAN

INVOKING SELKET FOR SUCCESS IN LIFE

Ritual Tools
· A statue of the Egyptian god Selket, an ornament of a dog, or the real thing (if he or she is happy to sit quietly by your side)
· High Priestess tarot card
· Scorpion ornament or picture
· One black and one white candle
· Lemon balm incense or oil to burn
· Ritual robes of white in velvet, silk, or pure linen with black sash or ribbon

Ritual Time
Waning to new moon.

Set your altar in a quiet part of your home and place the dog and scorpion ornaments on either side of the tarot card. Place one of the candles on either side of the symbols and light along with the incense.

Dressed in your robes, invoke the goddess by chanting as follows:

> "Oh powerful Selket, as you protected and guarded your peoples, let me honor your strong feminine spirit. Come with me as I tread the pathway of life. Enable me to sense deception and secrecy and fight that which will try to stand in my way, and help me to distribute the gifts I have been blessed with. Aid me in the following goals: [*state your requests here*]."

Conclude the ritual by snuffing out the candles and spending a while reflecting on what the goddess means to you. Honor the power of Selket to invoke the mysteries of life.

INVOKING SARAMA FOR LOVE

Ritual Tools

· A piece of gold cloth in any fabric
· Sprigs of ivy, pine needles, or oak bark
· An amulet or ring containing turquoise
· One red and one green candle
· A wand (of any material)
· Green agate and red snakeskin jasper stones
· A lamp to be lit by one of the lighted candles
· Ritual robes of red

Ritual Time

Near new moon.

Bathe and relax. Use rose-scented oil or rose moisturizer to calm your spirits.

Before you dress, lie down and visualize the power of the moon coming into your room and healing your body and mind. See a pure pink light entering your hands and filtering all through your body. As you dress, visualize your auric energy as a pink light surrounding your space.

Prepare your altar with the gold cloth and place the lamp as the centerpiece. Position all the other tools around the lamp, with one candle on either end of the altar, and light the candles. Then light the lamp.

Invoke the goddess Sarama by chanting the following:

> "Goddess Sarama, powerful Lady of her clan, inspire me with the dedication to purify my spirit, which I am capable of doing. Clear my mind's pathway to journey toward the goals I have chosen to achieve: [*state your goals here*]. Open the doors that will bring me loving energy, and allow my soul's mate to enter my life freely and willingly, knowing that our journey will bring us closer to our individual fulfillments. I open my path to the entry of this special person, and allow the Goddess to help me in designating the correct time and place."

Snuff out the candles and lamp. Dedicate the week to the goddess and wear the amulet or ring in her memory.

MEDITATION FOR NEW FRIENDS AND MATES

Relax and calmly visualize yourself at the seaside standing on a rock plateau with the sea gently lapping against the edge. The sky above is a soft dark blue with wisps of pink and orange as the sunset approaches.

Ahead of you is a small cottage resting against a high, strong wall of stone. Through the windows of this cottage you can see soft flames in a fireplace. Gently twirling smoke flows from the chimney.

You look at the front door. It is a thick double door with rich tones of brown and red wood. The handle is a beautifully carved dog's head.

You are now at the front door. As you place your hand on the handle to turn it, the door opens slowly and a figure greets you with smiling eyes and mouth. He takes your hand and seats you in front of the fire in a deep, red, velvety chair.

You look at each other and you know that he is asking you to share his home with you. Take your time, look around the room, study each object, and feel at one with the energy you are creating. You will know if this person is right for you.

The choice is always yours.

Cat Woman

THE NATURAL ENCHANTRESS

CHARMS AND SYMBOLS

Tarot card: The Star, which represents dreams and inspirations

Moon phase: Waxing

Celestial bodies: The moon

Herbs and plants: Willow, pussy willow, lily, camellia

Colors: All shades of cream, greens, pinks

Crystals and gemstones: Moonstone, cat's eye

Incense: Lemon balm, lotus

Lucky day: Monday

Lucky numbers: 2, 11, 20

Ritual colors: Whites, pinks

Ritual robes: Capes, gloves, and hoods in your colors, cat suits

Magickal symbols: Cats, sistrums, lynxes, rabbit paws (the rabbit and the cat have an esoteric connection; see below)

Goddesses: The virginal, the youthful

Theme song: "Year of the Cat" by Al Stewart

ASSOCIATED GODDESSES FOR THE CAT WOMAN

Bastet: Known as the "Cat Mother" or the "Little Cat," Bastet is an Egyptian goddess of love, celebration, and protection. She was usually depicted as having the body of a cat. Her cult was extremely widespread, and huge crowds attended her feast day. Her sacred instrument is the sistrum and musical instruments like the flute. The sistrum was used to frighten away evil spirits. Bastet was thought to be the embodiment of feminine power, wisdom, and love. She was prayed to for protection and luck. The worship of Bastet continued until the end of the fourth century. She was honored as the divine moon goddess.

Kaltes: The Russian rabbit goddess who was worshipped by the Siberian people. The hare (akin to cat energy) is her sacred totem. The rabbit is traditionally associated with the cycles of the moon, intuition, and enchantment.

Diana: The Roman goddess of the moon was regarded as the epitome of purity and maidenhood. Cats were her special totem animals.

Luna: Roman goddess of the moon connected with the waxing cycles.

POSITIVE TRAITS

graceful   well-groomed
intuitive   emotional
gentle   accepting
magical   laid-back
refined   humorous
loving   romantic
receptive   moderate
particular   charming
easy-going   aware
mysterious   entrancing

NEGATIVE TRAITS

studied   hypersensitive
weak   illusive
vain   critical
unrealistic   vacillating
fussy   lazy
deceptive   materialistic
dependent   sarcastic
clouded   calculating
jealous   envious
insecure   timid

FAMOUS CAT WOMEN

Lisa Kudrow · Jane Seymour · Kate Winslet · Fanny Brice · Edith Piaf
Natasha Richardson · Anjelica Huston · Angelina Jolie · Joan Crawford
Helen Hunt · Tina Turner · Drew Barrymore

CAT WOMAN'S NUMBER

1 Your elegance and natural flair will attract many admirers. You will have extra self-confidence and will succeed in a career in the public eye.

2 You are emotional and particularly receptive. You should follow a career in a highly personal field. Love is very important to you.

3 You have a great literary style and can be a first-rate writer. You love life and people, enjoy the arts, and need a free and easy lifestyle

4 You need a stable home and are capable of building it for others. You need to work in a structured style and you take your love affairs seriously.

5 You can be extremely alluring and will top the fashion stakes! Naturally restless, you need to express your creative side.

6 You have a very loving yet demanding nature. You need natural surroundings and work well with people.

7 Mystery and style combined! You may, however, be a lonely Kitty unless you practice balance in your life. You have a flair for investigation and research.

8 Your numbers increase your ambitious side. You will work hard to achieve your goals yet retain your sensitivity. Good combo for a human resource manager or a business-focused woman.

9 You can be a pioneering intellectual with a powerful creative side. You will thrive on challenges. Risk-taking may need curbing.

THE ENCHANTRESS!

Edith Piaf sang *"Chanson Bleue"* with passion and vulnerability. Such is the energy of the Cat woman: forever feminine, entrancing, and poignant.

The Cat woman naturally relates to the Moon Goddess as she is extremely sensitive and has a youthful, energizing personality. She is the natural femme fatale: alluring, yet springlike and virginal. Her feline grace and independence mark her immediately for attention, and she is adept at creating an aura of mystery as well as seduction.

The Cat woman loves the arts, naturally enjoys creativity, and is a wonderful performer. Her sensitive and powerful perceptions allow her to portray deep emotion in her work as an artist. She senses what her other animal sisters miss and uses this knowledge to her advantage.

Her natural inclination is to take the most diplomatic pathway, preferring avoidance to confrontation. For this reason, some see Cat women as insecure or weak. However, the Cat woman's strength often lies in her very passiveness, and she can often turn this to her advantage.

The great Egyptian goddess Bastet, who was venerated for centuries in her native land, always had the cat as her totem animal. Cats, too, were regarded as sacred and were often mummified by the ancient Egyptians as tokens of respect for the goddess. Bastet's attributes included intuition, healing, and the bringing of love to others. She is usually represented holding a sistrum, a musical instrument symbolizing rebirth and the cycles of life.

Take a look at the delicate features of Cat women Jane Seymour and Kate Winslet and you will begin to realize the power of the Cat's beauty. Chanteuse Fanny Brice reveals the enchanting and entertaining power that Cat women are capable of. Drew Barrymore expresses the Cat woman's versatility, while Angelina Jolie epitomizes the modern Cat woman's mystery and lithe gracefulness.

The Cat woman sometimes suffers from her sensitivities and should maintain a sense of balance and grounding in her life. Naturally sociable and friendly, she also has a detached side that can make her long for peace. It is very important for the Cat woman to have a quiet sanctuary to return to after her exertions in the outer world. The Cat woman also needs to be careful of taking things too personally as she tends to be rather thin-skinned.

In her own way, the Cat woman is quite pedantic about how she likes things to be done, and partners and friends can sometimes be exposed to a very fussy side! As she is prone to romance and idealism, the Cat woman usually prefers the dream to the reality of life. Learning to realize the importance of common sense can sometimes be a challenge!

In her life and vocation, the Cat woman displays many talents and is indeed a most versatile creature. While this is in many ways a lucky thing, it also tends to scatter her energies around, which may cause her to not achieve her potential or cause personal burnout. She is well advised to set aside time to pursue intellectual or creative pursuits despite challenges.

Of all the animal sisters, the Cat woman is the one that most thrives on support and approval. She greatly desires and appreciates close family relationships, which in turn help her to find herself and realize her full potential.

Despite her need for independence and occasional solitude, the Cat woman excels in an atmosphere of refined society. She is quite particular in her choice of associates and can sometimes appear rather snobbish. Her preferences are for the artistic and creative pursuits of life, and she is emotionally repulsed by vulgarity.

Her high standards, however, need to be tempered with reality. The Cat woman knows what she wants, but will not lower herself to become involved in scraps and fights. She may cut herself off from living life for fear of losing her ideals. Indeed, if she finds herself in a situation that to her is intolerable, she will turn and walk away rather than become involved with it. The Cat woman requires the achievement of her ideals, but needs to balance the unattainable with the attainable.

Her animal nature is one of the most gentle under natural circumstances, but this does not mean she is a coward by any means. The Cat woman can stand her ground, especially if she perceives you to have encroached upon her territory. To personal rebuffs and insults her usual defense is to affect an attitude of haughtiness and icy indifference. This can, however, turn to sarcasm and defensiveness if she is pushed too far. The Cat woman is keen to pick up on her opponent's weaknesses with her sharp critical streak.

The Cat woman needs to develop a sense of compassion and connection in life. Fostering closeness with her loved ones is very important as she has a great need for inner peace and may withdraw at times.

Her major challenges to face are her perfectionistic tendencies, the tendency to be hypercritical, refusing to face realities, and her deeply vulnerable ego. She also needs to watch a jealous and possessive streak in her energy, which threatens to damage her personal relationships if not curtailed. Nonetheless, her aura of freshness and entrancing beauty can be a perrrrfectly powerful charm, which will continue to captivate her audience no matter what her age!

CAT WOMAN AND LOVE

Love for the Cat woman can be a very heart-rending experience. Her sensitive, almost mystical nature, coupled with her natural perceptiveness and independence, makes for a creature that will be affected by love almost as powerfully as the beautiful character portrayed by Kate Winslet in *Titanic*.

Truly relating to the love goddess Bastet, the Cat woman brings her partner all the gifts of feminine mystique. She does not really like to chase her love object, and unlike her Monkey and Rooster sisters, she seldom sets out to aggressively woo her chosen one. She tends to prepare her love parlor with the appropriate bait, so to speak, and then wait patiently for her prey to walk in and succumb to her charms before she makes any captive pounce. However, this cool reticence can sometimes cause her to take a back seat in the love game.

As she is attuned to the hypnotic energies of the Moon Goddess, the Cat woman is often a little too fanciful in the way she sees a partner. Like all her animal sisters, emotional energy can affect her deeply, and she may fall victim to many unrequited love attractions where her subtle qualities are unappreciated. Fortunately for her, there are still a great many traditional mates out there who will enjoy her gentle enchantments and are confident enough to pursue her. Cat woman adores to be pursued!

The Cat woman's critical energy is one of her major challenges in love. She can exhibit quite a perfectionist streak. She must be careful not to scratch her perfectionist paws too sharply against her mate when he or she fails to live up to her (at-times) unrealistic expectations!

The Cat woman is a creative and refined wife who is stylish and inventive in the home environment. As a mother, she is not overly attracted to the messy side of

Cat Woman and Compatibility

Cat & Rat ♡	Oh no! Rat is far too slippery for Cat lady. She, in turn, will frustrate Rat.
Cat & Ox ♡♡♡♡	Can work if Ox is inclined to take some risks!
Cat & Tiger ♡	No, this one has too many power struggles between Cats.
Cat & Cat ♡♡♡♡	Good, as they can be very creative together. There is lots of mutual respect and purring!
Cat & Dragon ♡	Difficult because the Dragon can be very bossy and has a large ego.
Cat & Snake ♡♡♡	These two have a natural empathy. Very telepathic together!
Cat & Horse ♡	This is bound to have difficulties, as Horse is too energetic.
Cat & Goat ♡♡♡	Good team that will share concepts and ideas. They may write a novel or play in the country!
Cat & Monkey ♡♡	Can have an unusual relationship, but Cat will be kept on her paws! Monkey can never quite figure Cat out, but this may be fun.
Cat & Rooster ♡	Rooster displays "ego energy" and Cat will nod off to sleep.
Cat & Dog ♡	Hard because they are coming from different places.
Cat & Pig ♡♡♡	Good energy, rapport, and empathy likely.

♡♡♡♡ = excellent   ♡♡♡ = good   ♡♡ = fair   ♡ = difficult

domesticity or raising a child, but is very proud of her offspring all the same. Again, she needs to watch that her children are not subjected to her overcritical side though, as this will stifle them.

In the comic strip *Batman,* Catwoman is often shown as Batman's polar opposite. Catwoman portrays his enemy, but there is always an underlying attraction between the two. Catwoman is drawn to Batman's brilliance and intellect, and Batman, in turn, is attracted to Catwoman's feline power and sexuality.

This is a good analogy for the Cat woman in real terms. She needs a partner who will provide excitement and intellectual stimulation to balance that sometimes cool detachment. She needs a partner who is adventurous and even a bit of a risk-taker as she can become bored very easily in a mundane union.

In immaturity, the Cat woman can become caught up in various interesting liaisons. These do not usually last very long, however, as she quickly loses interest unless provided with a challenge.

Although she can suffer from a broken heart just like everyone else, the Cat woman normally is very resilient in this area and has a great capacity to move forward emotionally as she becomes more experienced. Her ideal mate would be someone who combines intellect with emotional maturity, and can cope with a sensitive, romantic lady who needs to be subtly appreciated.

CAT WOMAN AND HEALTH

A delicate nervous system and hypersensitive skin are two of Cat woman's vulnerabilities in health. She should place her health as a major priority as she can suffer periodic spells of various maladies.

Many of the Cat woman's issues can be avoided if she eats proper food and practices regular meditation. She has a need for regular and sustained exercise, and benefits from studying martial arts and yoga as well as various forms of dance. Like her cat animal friend, her body craves indulgent rest at times. She needs to stop skipping naps and overstimulating her senses with wild parties!

CAT WOMAN AND fINANCES

Finances are a bit of a necessary evil for the Cat woman, for she loves to indulge herself in a few luxuries from time to time. She is a careful planner, yet inclined to underestimate her financial value. The Cat woman should always seek to improve her position and not accept second best.

The Cat woman has quite a knack for accumulating valuable art pieces and antiques, and may even gain modest wins in the stock market. Her best investments are those she is attracted to, like jewelry and real estate. She also has a gift for running her own business.

CAT WOMAN AS A CHILD

Fey, feline, and endearing are the qualities that ensure the female Cat child will always charm. Possessing a naturally feminine energy, she will enjoy playing dress-up, wearing make-up, and will love to ensnare any stray mate. The Cat child's father will often be totally devoted to her charms.

Normally, the young Cat will be instantly attracted to creative pursuits. So money spent on educating her in music or theatre would be a wise investment. She may not be attracted to competitive or aggressive sports, but will instead feel drawn to develop her more receptive qualities. She is usually a rather clever scholar.

The Cat child is extremely sensitive, and her moods can swing quickly if she is not happy. As an adolescent she may be rather temperamental.

The Cat child is usually delicate, so her health must be monitored. On no account should she be subjected to prolonged stress or uncouth company as she has an allergy to vulgarity in all forms. She is normally affectionate and well-balanced otherwise.

CAT WOMAN AND CAREER

The Cat woman's artistic and creative sides help her to excel in a number of roles, including actor, dancer, and musician. Her finely tuned insights attract her to psychology and counseling, while her fashion sense and personal flair make her an excellent fashion designer or buyer. Her talents lie in any field that demands an eye for beauty, such as beauty therapist, antiques dealer, or home decorator and designer. Other fertile options are industries involving travel, hospitality, and public relations. She can also be a rather good private investigator.

The Cat woman is not really suited to clerical or administrative positions, although she can do a competent job in either. Cats should steer clear of any hands-on jobs like gardening, painting, kindergarten teaching, or any sort of manual labor–type careers. The typical fussy Cat woman is adverse to anything that involves getting herself messy or untidy-looking!

CAT WOMAN IN THE TWENTY-FIRST CENTURY

The Cat woman finds herself a valuable commodity in this time. Her sharp eye for detail and insight will make her a leader in the fashion and artistic fields, and she will be found in all manner of avant-garde occupations. She will excel in the creative arts, and we will see her continue to bloom as a writer, actor, producer, or in the public relations fields. The Cat woman will also find herself in the alternative therapy fields and will be interested in new forms of healing.

CAT WOMAN AND SPIRITUALITY

In medieval times, cats were always associated with witchcraft and the role of the familiar of witches. It was said that witches frequently chose to turn themselves into cats at will, and the belief was that cats themselves enhanced the power of magick workings.

Cats were a powerful part of Egyptian magick and spellcasting and were revered in sacred temples. Feline energy and the gods and goddesses are linked in almost every major culture in history from India through to the Middle East and Greece.

In Vietnam, the cat is considered an integral part of the zodiac, and in other parts of Asia it alternates with rabbit energy.

The Cat woman's energy naturally draws her to the world of the unseen and the enchanting. She is usually extremely sensitive, and has uncanny insights and powerful intuition, touched by a good dose of magickal charm! She is often psychic and possesses a powerful intuitive sense about her surrounds. She also has an amazing capacity to resurrect herself if she taps into her deep spiritual reserves.

The Cat woman naturally connects with sacred cat goddesses like Bastet and the Roman goddess Diana, who is the Roman version of the Greek goddess Artemis. Dianic rituals involving cats took place in temples in the Roman woods with a full moon overhead.

In understanding her animal self, the Cat woman begins to bring real power into her life. The rituals described below are designed to develop the Cat woman's natural affinity with her mystical being.

RITUAL WORK FOR THE CAT WOMAN

INVOKING DIANA FOR PROSPERITY AND GOOD FORTUNE

Ritual Tools
- Seven white candles
- A picture, photo, sculpture, or ornament of a cat
- A piece of moonstone and/or cat's-eye
- One stick of lotus or vanilla incense
- A small, white tablecloth
- A white or green ritual dress with a cape

Ritual Time

Near midnight on a full moon.

Choose a private place to create your altar to the goddess Diana with the above magickal tools. You may choose a place outside where the moonlight will touch the altar. Invoke the goddess Diana by first chanting her name seven times (Diana's sacred number).

Light the candles and incense and allow the atmosphere to gently build. Then, taking the moonstone and/or cat's-eye in hand, recite as follows:

> "Great goddess Diana, the sacred goddess of all cats, I invoke your power in my present life. I honor your grace and your mystery. I respect all that is pure and life-enhancing. I recognize my sacred cat spirit and seek to enrich the lives of those around me. To enable me to do this, I seek your assistance to focus myself on drawing positive energies into my life. As you merged with the cat spirit and in it found your power, may I, too, link with my sacred power."

After concluding the ritual and snuffing out the flame, take the moonstone and/or cat's-eye and bathe them in moonlight for seven nights. Then place on altar.

INVOKING BASTET FOR LOVE AND HAPPINESS

Ritual Tools
- Statue of Bastet or a cat
- A small willow twig or a lily flower
- Several leaves of parchment paper
- The Star tarot card
- One stick of rose incense
- One pink and one green candle

Ritual Time

Best performed under a full moon.

After bathing, prepare your altar in a quiet spot in the garden, on the patio, or under a window where you can see the moonlight. Place your tarot card, statue, candles, and lily or willow twig on your altar. Light your candles and incense and meditate on the perfection and light of the Star card. On the parchment paper, write all the characteristics you truly desire and need in a soul mate. Place the parchment under the statue.

Invoke the goddess Bastet to hear your petition by chanting the following:

"Bastet, goddess of love, celebration, and joy, empower me in my life. Guide toward me a subtle yet nurturing partner. Help me see clearly my pathway and needs to choose my rightful destiny."

As you snuff out the candles, have faith in the goddess to bring your wish to manifestation. Remain calm and be positive in your thoughts and actions to bring about good fortune to your own life and all those who are dear to you.

MEDITATION FOR CALM AND FOCUSING

Create a sacred place where you feel at peace and can enjoy some privacy.

Now imagine yourself sitting on a velvet cushion in the middle of a large, white hall with tall doors and splendid windows. You are seated under a fantastic chandelier, which glitters with clarity and intensity. Beyond the doors you can see the outline of a fabulous garden with a marble fountain bathed in moonlight. You love this room and feel safe here.

As you relax in this way, you notice a large, black cat enter the room from a door to the side of you. It comes directly up to you and rubs its tail against your lap. It is wearing a black velvet collar encrusted with three precious jewels: one is colored yellow, one is red, and the other is blue.

You bend down to have a closer look at the cat and notice her large golden eyes regarding you wisely. You feel a deep, telepathic connection with this animal. Somehow, you can understand what she is saying to you. The cat tells you to take the collar off her neck and examine it.

You look first at the yellow jewel. The cat communicates to you that the yellow jewel represents creativity and inspiration. You look next at the red jewel. Your animal friend tells you this jewel is the fire of passion. Finally you look at the blue jewel. The cat communicates this one is the most precious of all, for this represents your intuition. She also tells you that these jewels are her gift to you.

You thank the cat for her gifts and stroke her fur. She sits on your lap for a while as you meditate on the jewels and their meaning. You reflect on which areas of your life you would like to improve and how these precious gifts can help you. (Many insights will be revealed to you during this quiet time, so be ready to write them down when you come out of your reverie.)

You place the collar back on the cat's neck and put her back down on the floor. Taking the three jewels in your hand, you slowly walk out into the moonlit garden. Looking directly up at the stars, you feel a new sense of clarity and an understanding of your life. You know what actions you must take to progress toward your goals.

The black cat has followed you out. She sits purring at your feet. She seems to have a healing energy and you can feel this power work its magick on you.

Walking over to the fountain you see a cream-colored jewelry box directly in front of it. You place the jewels in it for safekeeping. The cat communicates to you that she will guard them for you, but that they are yours to keep.

When you are ready to come out of your meditation, bid your friend good-bye and slowly open your eyes. Immediately record any insights. Return to your private space, your jewels, and your special friend whenever you need to see them.

PART II

Sun Goddess Women

Dragon Woman
THE NATURAL QUEEN

CHARMS AND SYMBOLS

Tarot card:	All Queens, which represent feminine rulership and dominion
Moon phase:	Full
Celestial bodies:	The sun
Herbs and plants:	Angelica, hazel, St. John's wort, sunflower
Colors:	Reds, oranges
Crystals and gemstones:	Ruby, red agate, jasper
Incense:	Frankincense, sandalwood, benzoin
Lucky day:	Sunday
Lucky numbers:	1, 10
Ritual colors:	Reds, oranges, ruby
Ritual robes:	Silks, chiffon, organza
Magickal symbols:	Mirrors, wands, scepters, crowns
Goddesses:	Rulers and sun goddesses of most cultures
Theme song:	"Respect" by Aretha Franklin

ASSOCIATED GODDESSES FOR THE DRAGON WOMAN

Amaterasu: Sun goddess supreme of ancient Japan. Amaterasu symbolized compassion and love. Her divine power is linked to the imperial families of Japan. She is usually depicted as a radiantly beautiful woman exuding rays of energy and vitality. Her symbol is the mirror. She needed to witness her radiance in the mirror before she realized her power.

Pele: Hawaiian volcano goddess. She was renowned for her quick temper and vitality. She is said to have made fire by snapping her fingers.

Pachamama: This Peruvian goddess was portrayed as a dragon. Amongst the Inca she was revered as a goddess of fertility who ruled over all agriculture.

Saule: Russian sun goddess associated with fertility and power. She governed many areas of life such as childbirth, healing, and progress.

POSITIVE TRAITS

electric
generous
majestic
fiery
strong
commanding
attentive
kindly

charismatic
knowledgeable
wise
capable
dynamic
caring
compassionate
empathetic

NEGATIVE TRAITS

bossy
dominant
overbearing
arrogant
martyr
overactive
soft
irresponsible

edgy
destructive
jealous
aloof
emotional
obsessive
attention-seeking
vain

fAMOUS DRAGON WOMEN

Juliette Binoche · Dinah Shore · Wynonna Judd · Courtney Love
Isabella Rossellini · Julia Ormond · Roseanne Barr · Calista Flockhart
Courteney Cox · Sandra Bullock · Reese Witherspoon

DRAGON WOMAN'S NUMBER

1 You are commanding and energetic. You like to lead and will be very individualistic. Curb your temper.

2 You are a gentle and caring Dragon and need lots of encouragement. You have powerful intuition!

3 Versatile, communicative, and energetic. You would make a marvelous writer or speaker.

4 You need powerful goals and can help others obtain theirs. You are well-suited for the armed forces!

5 You have immense potential to excite and motivate others. A Dragon on the move!

6 Love and relationships are very important to you and you love to be leant on. Watch your moods.

7 Intuitive and sometimes a bit of a loner, you love to travel and contemplate life. A good explorer!

8 You can be very good at business, but somewhat extreme. Watch your health.

9 Intelligent and astute, you could be a pioneer or entrepreneur. Love is a dramatic affair in your life.

THE QUEEN!

Majestic, vital, alluring, and magnetic, the Dragon woman is the natural queen of the animal signs. Her presence is arresting, her desires powerful, and her appetite strong. She has many characteristics in common with her sister Tiger woman, but Dragon is less the hunter and more the ruler.

The Chinese consider the dragon to be a most auspicious creature and treat its symbol with respect and awe. Likewise, the Dragon woman fulfills herself only when she is worshipped accordingly. (My own view is that most Dragon women have spent a number of lives as ruling females and they must continue this energy in the present life.)

As mythical beasts, dragons were often depicted blowing fire or steam whilst protecting precious jewels or treasure. In Chinese myth, four dragon kings guard the four seas of the earth. In the same way, the Dragon woman has a considerable capacity to evoke destructive or protective energy, fear or admiration.

With her association to the goddess, the Dragon woman clearly relates most particularly to the sun goddesses. In a number of old cultures (notably Japan and Russia), goddesses were linked to the generative powers of the sun as well as the moon. The Dragon woman, therefore, evokes many of the qualities of the Sun Goddess, including the masculine energy associated with her.

In my experience, the Dragon woman is, on first impression, a quiet person—seldom loud or showy. On more intimate acquaintance, however, she displays the fiery bounce she is famous for!

As such, the Dragon woman often finds it extremely difficult to take a back seat in life or feel she can delegate her many tasks to anyone else. She never quite trusts the concept that others are as capable as her. She suffers from a classic Type A personality. She stresses and frets over events, assuming far too much responsibility and succumbing to serious fatigue. She does possess a sharp intellect, but unfortunately often does not realize this potential as she is too bound up with taking on the world's problems and has so many responsibilities.

The Dragon woman often sets herself up for the fall without realizing it. She can become mesmerized by her own myth of power to such an extent that she literally puts herself away in the dungeon of exhaustion. She may be running her own business, raising a family, earning extra income on the side, and caring for a relative as well.

Her personal belief that "no one else can do it quite as well as me" has a lot to do with her multifaceted lifestyle. She can suffer from this enlarged sense of capability and has trouble trusting others or accepting help when it's genuinely offered. The Dragon has a sense of protecting what she sees as her domain and can suffer insecurity when others take the lead.

The Dragon woman is a natural matriarch and leader in her family circle. The ancient cultures regarded the dragon as the great mother goddess of all matriarchies. She is as kind and helpful as she is overbearing and dominating!

Protective, defending, and complete in herself, the Dragon woman is often puzzled when she becomes victim to someone's envy and jealousy of her impressively capable pursuits. She faces life with a tenacious and serious valor and is willing to take on anything. It is difficult for her to understand why others do not feel the same way. Despite her enlarged ego, she really does have a sensitive heart and can experience deep periods of sadness when her good nature is misunderstood.

The Dragon woman is a born ruler grasping to take hold of the reins and start the race! However, as she matures, she learns to shine in her own light without necessarily taking over the stage as writer, actor, *and* director. Even she will, at times, admit she has taken on too big a load and begin to realize there is nothing wrong about seeking help at some stages in her life.

Although the Dragon will never be short of attention, she needs to learn to live a more moderate lifestyle. Otherwise she will not find the support there when she needs it. I have known many a Dragon woman to suffer alone in times of crisis because she has been too self-sufficient for her own good! Humans are meant to interact, help, and depend on each other. This is how we learn about ourselves and our special place in the universe.

The strong-minded and fascinating energy of a Dragon woman can never be forgotten once one is encountered! She is a creature of warmth and fascination with an out-of-this-world appeal.

DRAGON WOMAN AND LOVE

The Dragon woman falls in love hard! Love is the most powerful feeling she is capable of and she brings all her considerable drive to it. She is romantic, passionate to the extreme, and very physical in her love expressions.

She is drawn indiscriminately to romance and will most likely fall in love with the wrong type of partner at least once in her lifetime. She will undoubtedly be attracted to the unattainable, the weak, or the philanderer. She attracts this type easily, but will find it more difficult to shake such energies off!

Her personal charisma attracts men like bees to a blossoming flower. However, like the queen bee herself, the Dragon woman must exercise restraint with the quantity of bees she allows into her chamber.

Her radiant aura of self-assurance can have an entrancing effect and snares many a young mate. However, like Pele, the Hawaiian fire-breather goddess, the Dragon woman can become very angry very quickly if her object of desire denies her the rightful respect she demands. Serious damage can result from an angry Dragon!

This sign tends to need an earthy, security-minded partner. The Dragon woman is surprisingly easy to hurt and may suffer great loneliness due to her apparent indomitable strength and overpowering passions.

My own great-aunt, who was a Dragon lady, fell madly in love with a married man while traveling the seas when she was barely in her twenties. Vital, passionate, and attractive, she had many admirers. Once she had fallen in love with this man, however, her mind was made up. She was unable to move on and spent her days reliving the fantasy over and over again without fulfillment. The Dragon woman has a tendency to hide herself away in make-believe caves and pine for what was or might have been, just like poor Puff the magic dragon who mourned the loss of his young companion when he grew up and moved away. (Sadly, my aunt never married or had children, and left this life not long after her lover passed on, who stayed with his wife and family.)

The Dragon woman feels she is subject to her great passions and in this aspect relates to the goddess Pele. The myth of this awesome fire-creating goddess is deeply entrenched in the Polynesian cultures. In fact, it is still the center of a worshipping group of people in Hawaii. The Polynesians believe that the goddess Pele provides fire and light and all will be well if she is happy. However, legend has it that if the goddess has a fight with her heavenly lover, the earth will feel her displeasure and catastrophic events such as erupting volcanoes will occur.

Dragon Woman and Compatibility

Dragon & Rat
♡♡♡

Good basic compatibility as long as the Rat plays straight! Rat looks up to the Dragon's power here.

Dragon & Ox
♡♡♡

Yes! Ox has the earthiness Dragon requires. Dragon may stray from the routine Ox offers though.

Dragon & Tiger
♡♡♡♡

Powerful links. Tiger can tame her! Dragon needs the vitality Tiger can provide.

Dragon & Cat
♡

Difficult but tempting. The Dragon may find the Cat too fussy!

Dragon & Dragon
♡♡

Needs tolerance as this union can have too much smoke! Two Dragons may fight over the treasure.

Dragon & Snake
♡♡♡

Yes, if Snake controls that secrecy and does not stray from the watchful Dragon.

Dragon & Horse
♡♡

Dragon can help Horse reinvent his or her purpose. Dragon also finds the Horse sexy! Power struggles are likely, however

Dragon & Goat
♡

Difficult because Goat is really a bit too sensitive. They can be good together if Goat gets to lead.

Dragon & Monkey
♡♡♡

Monkey can teach her fun. Dragon will want the Monkey to behave though! Monkey fascinates Dragon.

Dragon & Rooster
♡♡♡♡

Good interchange of egos. These two are a thrilling, dare-devil team. A few arguments are likely, however!

Dragon & Dog
♡

Can be a bit too much for Dog. The Dog likes peace and having a Dragon is no recipe for that!

Dragon & Pig
♡♡♡

These two will support each other but Pig will not always submit to Ms. Dragon's fire. Dragon will enjoy her mate's sensuality though.

♡♡♡♡ = excellent   ♡♡♡ = good   ♡♡ = fair   ♡ = difficult

In the same way, the Dragon woman needs to become more vitally aware of her innate feminine force. She must respect it and learn to control its overpowering fire. Dragon needs to draw on the reserves of her philosophical mind, good sense of humor, and the acceptance of her spiritual path to more adequately cope with the good and the bad of life's passionate encounters. The journey will be much more palatable with fewer hot eruptions!

The Dragon woman has such powerful warmth and such a good heart that it is extremely tragic to see her lose her pathway. It appears that most Dragon women are fated to learn karmic lessons from the experiences they have through their love lives. But the Dragon woman is capable, if she chooses, to use these experiences (and the subsequent empowering knowledge that painful lessons teach us) to help others, just as the goddess Pele, in a symbolic sense, is believed to do by providing warmth and light to her people.

Dragon woman Courtney Love was left alone to bring up her daughter following the suicide of her partner. Even though she was battling her own emotional and physical addictions, Love was able to channel her innate strength and warmth to provide her daughter with a home that would give her a chance to grow up as happily as possible. Dinah Shore used her Dragon-woman passion to host a show for women that was loved by audiences for years.

Destiny provides the Dragon woman with the passion to rule, but this is often a secret to her until she gains the key to self-mastery. Once this is attained, she is able to unlock the door to her inner secret dungeon that holds all the power of her feminine potential. The respect and approval she seeks and the path to becoming a true legend in her own time lie just behind this door.

As a wife and mother, the Dragon woman is strong and in control of herself. She is commanding and formidable with her family. She requires, however, the inner fortitude of a truly sincere and strong-minded partner with a practical turn of mind. Although she will respect her partner, she will never let him or her totally take control. The perfect mate for a Dragon woman will know how to tread the delicate line of compromise between total submission and rigidity and will help her bring equilibrium to her life.

The Dragon woman will bestow tremendous generosity and support to an adoring and honoring mate. However, her innate fire can easily turn to destruction in a relationship where she feels unappreciated or dishonored. Watch out Dragon women partners, you may end up a burnt crisp!

DRAGON WOMAN AND HEALTH

The Dragon woman's health is normally excellent. However, her eagerness to accomplish many different pursuits and her reluctance to delegate tasks makes her vulnerable to nervous exhaustion, fatigue, and stress-related illness.

The Dragon woman has a rather finely tuned nervous system and ideally should regularly take time out to rest and relax. Paying close attention to diet and learning meditation is recommended. If she repeatedly neglects her body, she may develop kidney or stomach problems. Temper tantrums will have an adverse effect on her heart and lungs.

DRAGON WOMAN AND FINANCES

The Dragon woman is an ambitious woman and has the potential to be rich and powerful. She dislikes subordination in any field of life, and will naturally accumulate money as she works her way to a comfortable position in the workplace. Her only real weaknesses are being overly generous to loved ones or naive in relation to business schemes. Sound investments in stock, bonds, and property are good areas for her.

DRAGON WOMAN AS A CHILD

The Dragon child will climb Mt. Everest and discover the Congo! One Dragon child of my acquaintance had aspirations of being a flying doctor nun, much like the character played by Sally Field. Dragon girls have ambition and great idealism, but may experience a fair amount of self-doubt as a child, so try not to rain on her parade or you could frighten her.

Like all children, Dragon children need lots of attention. But remember: the Dragon child requires this in larger-than-usual doses and more frequently as she lives to be in the limelight!

Her imagination has wings, and like the flying dragon of mythology, it can carry her far away. Although this is often an enchanting quality, especially in the young, at some stage she should be introduced to more realistic images of life to give her good grounding for a more practical approach in adolescence. At the same time, encourage her active mind and natural ambition and make her aware that she can make a difference in the world, no matter how she chooses to do it.

DRAGON WOMAN AND CAREER

This woman is the type who needs to be self-employed or at least in an autonomous position. She loves power jobs where she is the head or in charge of an area, otherwise she will easily become bored. Good-sense career choices include lawyer, doctor, editor, policewoman, politician, and basically any position of authority and responsibility.

The Dragon woman will work her way up the ladder and usually has a clear career path mapped out in front of her. She is not suited to subordinate positions as she lacks the patience for them and will not last long in mundane or repetitive jobs either. If she chooses to run her own business, she would be wise to have a financial investor assist her as she can lack financial sense and be too extravagant at times.

DRAGON WOMAN IN THE TWENTY-FIRST CENTURY

If the Dragon woman masters her emotional side, she can contribute enormously to the position of women in the twenty-first century. Dragon women who build up their self-confidence in this period of time and develop the courage to shine will find themselves in demand as leaders. It would not be surprising if we see some Dragon woman president or head of state in the next few years. The Dragon woman plays for the big ones!

DRAGON WOMAN AND SPIRITUALITY

Many of my Dragon women clients are very spiritual. The dragon in Chinese mythology holds a very auspicious place in celestial schemes as the bearer of amazing power and intellectual abilities. The dragon symbol represents great power and courage in many cultures.

The Dragon woman often displays mediumship potential as she has a keen interest and genuine belief in the otherworld. She is usually ethical and pure-hearted in her religious energy, and needs color and drama in her private rituals.

As a goddess energy, she relates well to the sun goddesses and fire goddesses such as the Japanese sun goddess Amaterasu or, as mentioned previously, the Hawaiian volcano goddess Pele. Like Amaterasu, she needs to "see" her power before she can use it.

RITUAL WORK FOR THE DRAGON WOMAN

INVOKING PELE FOR SPECIAL PETITIONS

Ritual Tools
- A number of red and orange candles to create a firelight effect
- Patchouli incense for prosperity
- Gold-colored altar piece such as a gold-plated candleholder
- Queen of Wands tarot card
- A red robe specifically dedicated for your ritual work
- Writing sheet of parchment paper

Ritual Time

Full moon in Aries or Leo.

Generally the Dragon's energy is one of color and drama, so a private space where the Dragon woman can express herself is recommended.

Pele was an extremely powerful and fierce Hawaiian fire goddess and she could turn anyone who disappointed her to stone. She was subject to violent extremes of temper and sometimes fits of destruction. This energy relates to the power of the Dragon woman to be either a source of life or destruction.

Create your altar with the items listed above. Light the candles and incense and draw on the power of the goddess Pele by chanting the following:

> "I invoke the protection of this goddess in my everyday life. Allow me to understand my strengths and weaknesses and to work on them accordingly. I acknowledge my fire and power as a woman. I ask the goddess to assist me in [*state request*] and guide me in my life."

Write your request on the parchment paper and burn it with one of the five candles. Conclude the ritual by meditating on the power of the flame. When done, snuff out the candles.

INVOKING AMATERASU FOR LOVE

Ritual Tools

· Three red candles to represent the divine energies of the goddess
· Small quantities of ginseng, juniper, and lime (herbs ruled by the sun and said to energize love)
· A small gold ring purchased for the spell
· A valentine card made by yourself
· Rose and lavender incense
· A small piece of red-colored material
· Three red ribbons each about one foot (thirty centimeters) in length
· A red ritual robe or dress

Ritual Time

Full moon, preferably in Aries or Taurus.

First bathe yourself and dress in your robes to prepare your energy. Create your altar with the items listed above. Light the candles and incense and open the red material flat on the altar. Invoke the goddess as follows:

> "Powerful goddess Amaterasu, I invoke thy great loving energy and compassion into my life. I draw on your divine essence and request protection in my affections and emotions. I ask that you bring love into my life and that you allow me to discern my right partner.
>
> "I petition you to help me develop my intuition so that I will know when the right one is close. I seek not to collapse into my emotions but to embrace my great fiery spirit and harness the gift of light I have to give to others."

Conclude your ritual by wrapping the ring, love herbs, and valentine card in the red material and binding it together with the ribbons. Snuff out the flames and leave the items on the altar as a symbolic gift to the goddess and a reminder to you of its prayer.

MEDITATION FOR CALM AND FOCUSING

Imagine yourself at the seaside. You are standing on pure white sand feeling the grains between your toes. It is sunset and the sun is a brilliant red-orange ball on the horizon.

To your right across the dunes is a large cave. Something about this cave strongly attracts you. You like the idea of a place to which you can retreat from the world. You approach it and see that it is furnished and lit with many colored candles and clear, bright, luminous crystals of many hues. You can also see a large gold-framed mirror standing inside with a soft red couch in front of it. You want nothing more than to rest on this couch. It looks so comfy and inviting.

As you sit down you cannot help but notice that right in front of you is the mirror. It is full length and oval shaped. It seems to be beckoning you to look deep within it.

You look into the mirror and see your reflection bathed in the soft light of the cave. As you do this, you feel you have seen yourself for the first time. You notice your eyes and what they say about you, and you note the expression on your face. If you look closely, you can see your soul speaking to you from this reflection. Note what it is telling you about your life and yourself.

Allow no negative or unduly critical thoughts to surface. Your mirror is only there to help you understand yourself in a positive way. If you find yourself thinking of any particular challenges you are facing, resolve to meet them with courage and strength, knowing you have this power deep within yourself. You acknowledge that you love your life in the everyday world, but you also understand that you need peaceful times for spiritual reflection.

If you see other people or things of meaning to you in the mirror, remember them for future reference. Then spend some time enjoying and relaxing in your cave. Go over your life at the moment and meditate on any area you need to feel more empowered in, remembering that self-knowledge is the key to true empowerment. This magickal mirror can help you understand yourself by allowing you to reflect quietly. By meditating regularly, you will find you are able to live your life with new understanding and ease.

When you are satisfied, rise, snuff out the candles, and by the light of the crystals in the cave, go out onto the beach in what is now the early evening light.

Open your eyes. Feel relaxed and calm. You can return to your mirror and secret cave whenever you need to have this time to yourself.

Rooster Woman

THE NATURAL DIVA

CHARMS AND SYMBOLS

Tarot card:	The Sun, which represents the life energy of its creative aspects
Moon phase:	Waxing to full
Celestial bodies:	The sun
Herbs and plants:	Daffodils, sunflowers
Colors:	Gold, yellow, orange
Crystals and gemstones:	Garnet, citrine, amber
Incense:	Frankincense, citrus, lemon
Lucky day:	Sunday
Lucky numbers:	1, 10
Ritual colors:	Gold, yellow, amber
Ritual robes:	Shiny satin, cloth of brocades, embroidery
Magickal symbols:	Peacocks, the phoenix, storks, roc birds, feathers, boas, masks
Goddesses:	The adorned, flamboyant, the love goddess, the show woman
Theme song:	"Come Fly with Me" by Frank Sinatra

ASSOCIATED GODDESSES FOR THE ROOSTER WOMAN

Xochiquetzal: Sexually alluring Aztec goddess who is referred to as the "Beautiful One." She was the goddess of the arts and entertainment and was renowned for her associations with love, fertility, and motherhood. Young women often braided their hair to symbolize the quetzal plume in her honor. Her symbols were the marigold and the dove.

Maat: Egyptian goddess of divine justice. She is always portrayed with feathers as symbols of the lightness of the spirit. She was usually depicted as a female with an ostrich feather on her head.

Pomba Gira: Brazilian goddess of extroversion and gaiety. Pomba Gira is often depicted in bright, colorful garments with a red carnation in her hair.

Uzume: Japanese goddess of happiness and dance. She was also linked with protection and wealth.

POSITIVE TRAITS

humorous	ambitious
bold	flamboyant
risk-taker	driven
curious	friendly
literate	assertive
leader	emotional
excitable	vivacious
desirable	determined
confident	articulate

NEGATIVE TRAITS

egocentric	drama queen
hasty	dominant
nosy	vain
overbearing	inconsiderate
nervous	indiscriminate
promiscuous	argumentative
ruthless	approval-seeking
needy	overconfident
agitated	bossy

fAMOUS ROOSTER WOMEN

Joan Collins · Cate Blanchett · Catherine Zeta-Jones · Britney Spears
Minnie Driver · Goldie Hawn · Renée Zellweger · Melanie Griffith
Bette Midler · Priscilla Presley · Dawn French · Joan Rivers · Kim Novak
Anna Kournikova · Yoko Ono · Ellen DeGeneres

ROOSTER WOMAN'S NUMBER

1 Bird of the moment, you know no fear. Take it easy though; you need inner peace and sometimes step on too many toes.

2 You seek your other half with drive. Watch those powerful emotions.

3 You are a natural for the stage or the dramatic arts, but you sometimes compromise too much and you need to practice self-control.

4 Organizer Rooster! You like to be in charge and be direct. You take things to extremes though, so be moderate.

5 Alive, electric, and formidable, use your energy wisely. Love affairs are powerful, but you bore very easily.

6 You have everyone's best interest at heart but can be too demanding. Learn to step back and cultivate detachment.

7 Sensitive and a little touchy, you seem a bit of a loner for a Rooster. Seek spiritual development and lighten up.

8 Businesslike and disciplined, you are a bit of a pressure cooker for a Rooster! You can be frustrated emotionally, so beware of workaholic tendencies.

9 Go-get-'em Rooster! You can be extremely successful at teaching or guiding others. Develop that intellect—it's powerful!

THE DIVA!

Bouncy, bold, and adventurous, the Rooster lady loves to be cock of the walk. She is self-confident, sassy, and sparkling, and she has the vitality and power to attract attention, flattery, and admiration no matter what her age!

A Rooster woman needs and demands your attention. I have named her the "natural diva" because whether she is a professional performer or not, she creates a lot of drama! She usually sees herself as the lead player and sometimes forgets the supporting cast.

Her love of life is legendary, and she must either have a partner or be dreaming of one. The Rooster woman struts across the stage of life with brilliance and daring. She does not, however, always fulfill all of her grand passions.

Although endearing, talkative, and possessing personality-plus, the Rooster woman suffers from vanity, overconfidence, and occasional myopia. She is more of a Sun than a Moon Goddess type being direct, competitive, and assertive as opposed to reflective and considerate. As her yang energies are greater than her yin, she tends to walk over or on people. She does this not from malice, but with a sense that she is the leader and boss.

The Rooster woman suffers from a great deal of naivety and is truly disappointed when others react to her domination. She believes she is a natural-born leader and does not understand why others do not just follow her. She needs to learn the power of effective management or she will often be left alone in her personal progress.

In the Rooster woman, the ego is well developed, which leads to success. What she also needs to learn is that self-absorption can lead to failure. Many Rooster women seek spiritual counseling or guidance in order to look deep within their own self. Usually troubles in the love-life area bring them to counseling. It is, however, problems of a deeper level that often need to be looked at and the Rooster must allow for introspection if she desires wisdom.

If the Rooster woman can learn to balance her ego side, she can use her marvelous creativity and showiness to her advantage. Her fine sense of humor can almost always save her. Rooster women such as Goldie Hawn, Bette Midler, and Joan Rivers are classic examples of the glitter of the Rooster personality. Catherine Zeta-Jones commands attention, as does singer Britney Spears and Renée Zellweger. Rooster women in the creative arts invariably shine with their comedic talents and personality!

Part of every day for the Rooster woman should be devoted to personal meditation. A number of Rooster women have explained to me that they have a great deal of difficulty meditating as they find the inner focus difficult to achieve. Yet it is important for the Rooster to actively practice calming and healing inner work. Yoga, meditation, and gentle breathing can soothe her aggression and anxiety.

The Rooster's relationships with her sister animal signs are rather complex. She needs someone to talk to, but finds it difficult to balance an equal exchange of ideas. Until she reaches maturity, the Rooster will dominate most conversations, finding her own life the most fascinating. Her listener will have glazed eyes, but the Rooster will not always see this.

The Rooster is an intensely competitive sign and loves to be the first in everything she undertakes. Again, she must practice temperance in her energy in this regard and learn to play second fiddle on the odd occasion. Her need to perform should be channeled into creative activities that absorb her ego. Then her private life can be calmer and her relationships more balanced.

The Rooster woman's terrific energy and vitality are so life-enhancing it is a pity when she does not realize her real potential. The Rooster certainly does not have to end up tomorrow's feather duster if she is wise to her own power.

ROOSTER WOMAN AND LOVE

Fiery, direct, and articulate, the Rooster loves to chase and capture, often easily out-running her female competitors. More forward than the Snake woman and with a self-assurance that is well defined, she surveys the available talent and makes her selection with purpose. She is a very sexual animal sign and needs plenty of passion.

She loves to boast about her captures and talk about her conquests. Most Roosters tend to be promiscuous in youth and jump impulsively at love. Not suited to a solitary lifestyle, the Rooster woman needs the attention and challenge of an intelligent and firm mate. Unfortunately, in the early part of her life, she tends to fall for superficial flirts who win her heart with false flattery. As she

Rooster Woman and Compatibility

Rooster & Rat ♡♡	Can be a winning combo if Rat stays focused on their relationship, which requires Rooster to be imaginative and maintain Rat's interest!
Rooster & Ox ♡♡♡	Yes, Rooster can respect Ox. The Ox can be strong and self-assured.
Rooster & Tiger ♡	This one will have its difficult moments, as Tiger is a very demanding partner.
Rooster & Cat ♡♡	Good natural empathy, but Cat is a little too sensitive at times.
Rooster & Dragon ♡♡♡♡	Very good; Rooster can express herself here. Dragon has no fear of Rooster overshadowing his or her sun.
Rooster & Snake ♡♡	Snake is a little too slippery for the direct Rooster, but there is attraction here.
Rooster & Horse ♡♡	The Horse needs a lot of freedom and Rooster may get insecure.
Rooster & Goat ♡♡	Maybe, but Goat likes quiet thought and Rooster needs excitement.
Rooster & Monkey ♡♡♡	Lots of fun and cheeky exchanges likely here. The Monkey adores bold Rooster.
Rooster & Rooster ♡♡	These two can have fun together as they make the feathers fly every time they connect. Egos can also collide though.
Rooster & Dog ♡♡♡	A solid match for both parties here. The Dog really warms to the Rooster's fair-play attitude and mutual admiration will develop.
Rooster & Pig ♡♡♡	Pig will let Rooster lead. Rooster will enjoy the focus that Pig gives the relationship and a merry time will be had.

♡♡♡♡ = excellent   ♡♡♡ = good   ♡♡ = fair   ♡ = difficult

matures, however, the Rooster develops discernment and makes better choices based on depth and sincerity.

Her main challenges in love are forgetting about her partner's needs while pursuing her own career and family interests, developing competition with a partner, and refusing to face facts about failed love affairs. The Rooster, despite her apparent confidence, suffers very profoundly if she is neglected or overlooked in the love stakes. She is not prepared for failure in her life partner choice, so a divorce or separation from a mate who has moved on can be extremely devastating for her and she will not easily recover. The Rooster woman needs to relax a little in her life, leave her dramatics for the stage, and bring home some peace.

The Rooster woman needs a calm, grounded partner and not a playboy who will compete for attention. With such a mate she can achieve happiness. At the same time, she needs to nurture her loved one and remember the little things that keep a relationship alive. This she needs to balance with an often-hectic career and social lifestyle.

As a wife and mother, the Rooster can be demanding and energetic. She has a need to temper her bossiness. She is extremely proud of her offspring and takes every opportunity to show them off. She sometimes needs to focus on understanding her children's sensitivities. However, as she is so much fun as a parent, her children usually adore her.

ROOSTER WOMAN AND HEALTH

Health is not usually of much interest to the Rooster woman. Her natural vitality is powerful, so she usually uses it! This does not mean, however, that she can neglect her health, particularly in terms of regular gynecological and physical checks. She has good general health, but lack of attention to preventative measures can take its toll over a period of time.

Most Roosters have a pretty hot temper, which can lead to chronic stress-related illness. The desire to always be number one may affect her mental and emotional balance.

ROOSTER WOMAN AND FINANCES

The Rooster woman has the capacity to make quite a lot of money. However, her preoccupation with keeping up with the Joneses means she will overspend to maintain this status. She needs a good financial plan and should curb her expensive tastes.

If she fails in business, she usually has the fortitude to begin again. She tends to have problems with female associates and should be careful with whom she associates in business.

ROOSTER WOMAN AS A CHILD

Vibrant and sassy, the Rooster child commands your attention. She loves to compete and will often get involved in active enterprises of the mind and body. Her communication skills will also be well developed and positive.

She will have many liaisons in a turbulent adolescence. She needs lots of affection and approval of her numerous talents, and she loves to have goals in life. As an adolescent she is quite headstrong and inclined to too many parties, clothes, and adornments. Although she has scholastic aptitude, she may wander away from her studies. Strong encouragement to stay at school may be needed.

ROOSTER WOMAN AND CAREER

The Rooster woman will love her career if she seeks employment opportunities in work where she can be her own boss. Fields she loves include public relations, advertising, the arts, media, journalism, acting (of course!), and interior design. She is also a good entrepreneur or legal expert. She excels in any leadership-type role! Her worst career choices are subordinate roles or mundane repetitive jobs.

The Rooster woman can easily become scattered in her energies. Therefore, she needs to focus on developing expertise in her chosen field if she is to succeed.

ROOSTER WOMAN IN THE TWENTY-FIRST CENTURY

The Rooster woman's success in her career is almost assured, and her natural drive and enthusiasm makes her a valued member of many societies. Her main challenge in the twenty-first century is really getting in touch with her deeper spirituality.

The Rooster woman can be so worried about the external values of the world, such as having the perfect mate or being the most successful company director, that she neglects the goddess within for a long time, usually to her detriment. As a result, she may find the next few years of this century to be somewhat disappointing unless she pays attention to her spiritual side as well. Taking time out for her spiritual development—unrelated to material accomplishment—is a major challenge to the Rooster but an important necessity in the twenty-first century.

ROOSTER WOMAN AND SPIRITUALITY

Honored as a sacred and powerful deity of sexuality and protection, the Aztec goddess Xochiquetzal also presided over all craftspeople and artisans. At the pinnacle of the Rooster woman's evolution, her spiritual energy is, like this goddess, a phoenix; it can be reborn again and again, always eternal and refreshing. The ancients associated the bird with the journey of the soul or the spirit to the afterlife. According to legend, the phoenix was said to return every five hundred years to be reborn as a gift of life. The following ritual invokes the power of resurrection that the phoenix represents.

RITUAL WORK FOR THE ROOSTER WOMAN

INVOKING XOCHIQUETZAL FOR SPECIAL PETITIONS

Ritual Tools
· Different colored feathers from favorite birds and pictures and ornaments of birds
· Phoenix statues or ornaments placed on a personal altar
· Orange candles and rose incense or oils to burn
· Ritual robes of orange or red
· Flowers of orange or red
· A mask, preferably feathered
· Soft music

Ritual Time
Early evening of the full moon.

Before the ritual, bathe yourself in your favorite oils. Place everything on your altar. Dress in your ritual robes and don mask. Light the candles and incense and play soft music in the background.

Invoke the goddess Xochiquetzal as follows:

> "Oh great goddess, I invite your power in my ritual. Natural giver of life and beauty to the Aztec peoples, I call on you to lend me your beauty and your flowering goddess energy. Enable me to use my natural energy and drive to achieve my goals [*state your personal goals now*]. I ask for your help in moderating my extreme self. Teach me that the external world is only a reflection of my inner power. I respect the beauty of the spirit over all that is in front of me."

Conclude the ritual by snuffing out the candles and incense. Dedicate the feathers on your altar to the goddess or wear the feathers in your hair in celebration of her benevolence.

INVOKING MAAT FOR LOVE

Ritual Tools

· Rose incense
· Red roses
· Red candles
· A gift for the goddess (this can be a symbolic amulet or piece of jewelry)
· A picture or statue of the goddess
· Ritual robes of red or pink

Ritual Time

At dusk of a full moon.

Prepare an altar with the items listed above. Dress in your robes and light the incense and candles. Meditate on the pleasures of life and love. Visualize yourself seated in a circular pergola and view all the open arches that lead out to a vast garden filled with birds and beauty and color. Imagine a figure surrounded in purple light in front of you and invoke the goddess Maat as follows:

> "Goddess, I seek balance and peace in my emotional life. Help me to rise above my passions and match me with a powerful and well-balanced soul mate. I ask for a partner that does not just flatter me, but also offers sincerity and commitment. For my part, I vow to go beyond appearances and status to the soul beneath. Thank you, goddess."

Snuff out the candles at the conclusion of your ritual. Honor her by wearing the gift dedicated to her and burning a candle for her each month on the full moon.

MEDITATION FOR CALM AND FOCUSING

Now calm and relaxed, imagine yourself seated in the middle of a beautiful, circular, white wrought-iron pergola. Imagine the pergola as big as you want.

This pergola has four wide arches forming the walls. Entwining the arches is soft green ivy mixed with wild roses and jasmine. You can smell the jasmine and rose perfume mingled with the soft warm breeze gently blowing against your skin. Surrounding the pergola is an immense garden; all you can see is grass and tall trees for miles.

You look up at one of the arches and standing there is a peacock, its feathers outstretched and brilliantly colored with translucent shades of blue and green. It looks at you and bows its head in acknowledgment of your shared soul and journey. It is telling you to look at the power of your unique self and shine this individual inner confidence outward.

To the next archway you see another bird; a white dove with eyes so red they look like exquisite rubies. This bird, too, bows its head to you. This dove represents the part of you that searches for peace and harmony. It is telling you to remain calm and thoughtful in times of stress.

The third arch presents a tiny gray swallow, its delicate feet perched gently on a fallen ivy twig. It tweeters a fond "Be brave, my friend" to you. The swallow is all that is childlike and innocent in you. It is telling you to hold on to your childish dreams and do not fear you will ever lose yourself to disappointment for "I am tiny, but I can fly fast and swiftly to anywhere I choose and take my dreams with me."

Turn now to the final arch. There standing tall and upright is a fine, handsome rooster. Its large feathers are a striking red and black. Its feet firmly stand on the floor and its eyes, strong and intense, look at you as if looking at a mirror. It says to you, "You will not always have control over what happens to you, but you do have control over how it affects your life and future. Your disappointments can only affect you in the way you let them.

"Only you can decide how life will teach you, and only you hold the power to succeed in your dreams. You are strong and capable of many joys, but learn to let go the temptation to always try to take control when it is wiser to let others (or a higher power) tell the story."

Gently come out of your meditation. Carry the beauty of the birds with you in your everyday life by looking at them as familiars or guides when you see them.

PART III

Earth Goddess Women

Pig Woman
THE NATURAL PROTECTRESS

CHARMS AND SYMBOLS

Tarot card:	The Emperor, which represents power and protection
Moon phase:	Waxing to full
Celestial bodies:	Venus
Herbs and plants:	Rosemary, sage, thyme, lavender
Colors:	Blue, purple, pinks
Crystals and gemstones:	Rose quartz, lapis lazuli
Incense:	Violet, rose, frankincense
Lucky day:	Friday
Lucky numbers:	6, 24
Ritual colors:	Violet, rose shades
Ritual robes:	Soft natural fabrics
Magickal symbols:	Hand of Fatima, pigs, the cornucopia, willow branches, pine cones, the ankh
Goddesses:	The protector, the Mother Earth
Theme song:	"The Power of Love" by Céline Dion

ASSOCIATED GODDESSES FOR THE PIG WOMAN

Demeter: The Greek goddess of the earth and mother to Persephone. Demeter was heartbroken when she lost her daughter to the underworld. Demeter represents qualities akin to the earth's richness, protection, and strength. She is sometimes shown as the goddess of corn, signifying the wealth of the earth.

Fortuna: The Roman goddess of plenty and fortune. Fortuna was often portrayed with wreaths and coins and was invoked for protection and prosperity by the ancient Greeks as well. Fortuna was the Roman manifestation of the Triple Goddess. She was associated with the Wheel of Fortune, later given the name Lady Luck. Her Roman name is believed to have been a derivative of *Vortumna* ("She Who Turns the Year" or the "Great Mother").

Kwan Yin: The beautiful Chinese goddess of motherhood, compassion, and mercy. Kwan Yin is often pictured with many arms to indicate her considerable powers for rescue. She is also known as the "Lady Who Brings Children."

Isis: The Egyptian mother goddess. Isis was considered to be one of the most powerful deities in Egyptian religion. Her cult spread all over the world. She was worshipped both as a magickian and a protectress. She is often portrayed with outstretched wings, which symbolize her influence.

POSITIVE TRAITS

kindly	commanding
generous	interested
strong	loving
well-meaning	practical
open	motherly
nurturing	ambitious
protective	determined
attentive	concerned
talented	humorous
life-loving	sensual
enduring	intense

NEGATIVE TRAITS

patronizing	unwise
overbearing	smothering
naive	domineering
territorial	possessive
scattered	greedy
bossy	interfering
unimaginative	overemotional
arrogant	ruthless
devouring	bawdy
wallowing	martyr
addictive	social climber

FAMOUS PIG WOMEN

Hillary Rodham Clinton · Nigella Lawson · Sarah Ferguson
Julie Andrews · Winona Ryder · Marie Osmond · Jenna Elfman
Shannen Doherty · Camilla Parker-Bowles · Paula Yates
Marie Antoinette · Christina Applegate · Ginger Rogers

PIG WOMAN'S NUMBER

1 A vital, energetic Pig who is a natural show-woman. Loves to be in the limelight.

2 Sensitive and intuitive Pig who loves to be in love but may lack self-esteem at times.

3 Pig lady with plenty to say! Needs inspiration. Can be marvelous communicator or writer.

4 Grounded and sometimes stubborn, this Miss Piggy needs room to roam and has great endurance.

5 Alert and adventurous. Magnetic Miss Piggy with a silver tongue. Watch for restlessness here.

6 Caring and extremely cozy. A Pig lady who needs a warm and affectionate hearth!

7 Empathetic, talented, and creative, but beware of too much dreaminess and lack of focus blocking your potential!

8 Drive, ambition, and achievement describe the personality of this go-getting Piggy! Watch greedy tendencies though.

9 A leading light, a great teacher or counselor Pig.

THE PROTECTRESS!

The passionately protective Pig woman holds incredible reserves of power within her. Direct, intense, and territorial, she evokes the mother goddesses like Kwan Yin and Demeter as well as the fierce energy of the protector goddesses. She is usually a very giving, generous woman who sincerely cares for others and looks after them with honest feeling, often putting herself second. She loves her family, and believes she knows what is best for them.

The Pig woman loves being a mother to all and obtains immense satisfaction from being of service to others. Pig woman Hillary Rodham Clinton has sought to represent her electorate in the U.S. Senate while Sarah Ferguson donates her time to charity work.

Although capable of marvelous achievements, the Pig woman's greatest Achilles' heel is succumbing to more wily characters than herself. As a caring woman, she often takes people and circumstances at face value. This quality, while charming, leaves her open to the subtle manipulation of others. There are many who will take advantage of her natural trusting disposition and lack of character discernment.

The Pig woman is well-meaning and displays this quite strongly and obviously. This outright straightforwardness may be resented as insistent interference. Unfortunately, the Pig does not see this effect on others. This is because in her mind, the Pig is the only one who can set things to rights!

Several Pig ladies of my acquaintance refer to themselves as moral watchdogs for the rest of us. It is in the Pig woman's makeup to help people and she has natural self-confidence. She must be careful, however, that this same strength does not lead to her downfall. Although she seldom means to, her anxiety to take care of others can easily cross the line into domination. Her "mother-knows-best" attitude is okay for raising children, but adults won't take it as tolerantly!

Surprisingly, many Pig ladies complain that they are weighed down with too much responsibility or that their mate or loved ones have taken too much of what they do for granted. In truth, it is usually the Pig lady herself that has created this scenario by giving the impression that she wants to take more on board and is happy to do so! Temperance is a major lesson for Ms. Piggy.

The Pig woman is a sensual soul and finds it difficult to deny herself most of life's pleasures. Occasionally it must be said that Madame Pig can be a little greedy and even territorial. The Pig lady needs to learn when to share with others.

Although usually thought of as gentle and self-sacrificing, the Pig woman is undeniably capable of standing up against adversaries if threatened in any significant way. Visualize the charging power of a wild boar and you've got some notion of a Pig lady in anger and on guard! In the same way, she is capable of a great deal of emotion if someone she loves is hurt or threatened, and she can go on quite a voracious rampage to protect and revenge them.

This does not mean that she is naturally a mean or spiteful lady, but the Pig woman can suffer very deeply from the emotions. She needs to study psychology and human relations to help her detach from her powerful feelings. She should also appreciate the power of the mind and its positive and negative uses.

The Pig lady must be careful not to give in to dark mood swings and anger, as she may become self-destructive and lose her balance. On no account should she lean toward alcohol or drugs to console her in this regard. It is important for her to maintain a feeling of worth in her life, which can be best achieved with a wide network of friends. The Pig lady is a most loyal, sustaining, and loving person, and caring relationships are natural for her. Pig woman Paula Yates suffered from severe depression in her short life after the loss of her partner and her subsequent death deprived us all of her marvelous creativity and wit.

The Pig woman has a serious aptitude for learning and should pursue academic interests to further develop her intellectual strengths. Many Pig ladies I have had the pleasure of meeting are potently intelligent women who have succeeded in all areas of professional endeavors.

Diligent and ambitious, Pig women can be of great value to employers as they never shirk responsibilities. However, in her career, as in all other parts of the Pig woman's life, she needs to practice a degree of discretion. Her natural instinct is to take over and correct the problems single-handedly, but not all her coworkers will appreciate being overrun!

Learning to participate as part of a team is an important lesson for the Pig woman. She must learn to give and take and also watch her temper! However, when she achieves a sense of balance, she can really shine in a position of leader or co-coordinator. Others will truly be inspired by her generosity and energy.

PIG WOMAN AND LOVE

The Pig woman is one of the greatest lovers of the animal signs! She is nurturing, caring, and extremely faithful; qualities that give her a full score in the love stakes. Her main challenges in love are a tendency to dominate her partner, undervalue her own worth, and allow her extreme emotions to take control. If she can balance these aspects of herself, the Pig lady can prove one of the most delicious of mates, being sensual, humorous, and profoundly feminine.

The Pig lady's partner invariably experiences her powerful maternal side, basking in her loving attentions. The Pig woman must, however, learn to give and take in love. The overmothered partner may feel more like he or she is being devoured with love than nurtured!

The Pig woman would do well to learn about the multiple facets of the mother goddesses that she is akin to. She needs to realize that the best mothers are the ones that care for a person, but also respect that person's need to evolve his or her own personality. This same lesson applies to the handling of her own children.

When young, Pig ladies often find themselves in relationships with mates who desire a mother-type figure to give them the sort of security and emotional support that they have been deprived of in their own mother-child experience. The Pig woman is often willing to play this role to a point. She becomes disillusioned with a partner who ends up taking her motherly love for granted, even though she will tolerate it for long periods.

As the Pig lady matures, she learns to expect a mate to nurture her too. The perfect mate for her is a devoted family-type who is willing to share all the responsibilities that raising a solid family entails. If the Pig woman is lucky, she will find such a partner early in her life. If not, she can be prone to stay in an unsatisfactory partnership rather than lose her perceived security. She must, however, learn to move on when one is not right and mature past her naivety. Most Pig ladies I have met do not relish the thought of singledom, and instead much prefer to be in a partnership, even if this is not the best scenario.

Pig women are loyal and not inclined to stray, but their sensuous nature does sometimes lead to a few lovers! When properly settled, the Pig lady makes a wonderful wife and mother (though she may be quite strict with her young piglets!).

Pig Woman and Compatibility

Pig & Rat
♡♡♡

A good match is likely here as these two can respect each other. Much intellectual stimulation can occur, though they both need to avoid taking risks.

Pig & Ox
♡♡♡♡

Ox will protect Pig and give a double dose of security to a solid union. Both individuals love to nurture each other.

Pig & Tiger
♡♡

These two will clash too much. Tiger has powerful ideas of right and wrong and may upset the more moderately geared Pig.

Pig & Cat
♡♡♡

Peace is likely here; these two are well matched with similar needs. The Cat likes to be spoiled and the Pig will try to spoil the Cat!

Pig & Dragon
♡♡♡

Great team! Dragon is well meaning and appreciative of Pig lady's tenderness and nurturing instinct.

Pig & Snake
♡

Oh no! Pig will suffer with the Snake's indirectness. Can be creative partners, though, if they learn to communicate.

Pig & Horse
♡♡

Can be okay if Horse slows down the gallop to a canter. Pig helps the Horse ground those impossible dreams.

Pig & Goat
♡♡♡

A respectful combination. Both like peace and quiet and the well-appointed home. This team can produce a work of art.

Pig & Monkey
♡

Monkey tricks Pig, Pig dominates Monkey, and clashes are frequent.

Pig & Rooster
♡♡♡

Lots of hijinks are likely here, but nothing to stop them enjoying the ride.

Pig & Dog
♡♡♡♡

A devoted pair, these two are amiable and contented. Lots of domestic bliss will be their lot. They value the same things.

Pig & Pig
♡♡♡♡

Great vibes. They'll be connected, devoted, and family-minded.

♡♡♡♡ = excellent   ♡♡♡ = good   ♡♡ = fair   ♡ = difficult

PIG WOMAN AND HEALTH

The Pig woman tends to do things to the extreme. She needs to watch stress and her diet as her stomach is very sensitive and may play up when she is under pressure. She should eat plenty of fresh vegetables and avoid overindulging in rich foods and alcohol. Pig women and substance abuse are also a very destructive combination, so she would be wise to note this early.

The Pig lady truly benefits from regular health checks. Key areas of potential concern are fluid balance, stomach problems, and thyroid. She should avoid excessive use of any drugs and drink only in moderation. Also, meditation and yoga calm her down and provide a necessary balance to her busy lifestyle.

PIG WOMAN AND FINANCES

Finances prove something of a challenge to most Pig ladies who will normally be very generous in this department. Although she may earn a good salary, she will spend it and cannot resist the occasional treat! She loves the best in food and wine and enjoys spoiling her family and friends with gifts. Her desire to spend big may lead her to overdraw her resources. The Pig woman should invest in sensible saving options and get herself a large piggy bank to maintain her generous flamboyance!

PIG WOMAN AS A CHILD

The little Miss Pig is a very caring child who is likely to take over the welfare of her siblings at an early age. She is a little bossy and stubborn, although her winning smile and warm heart will more than make up for these aspects of her character.

Miss Piggy usually enjoys learning and devours books like candy. She will take a great interest in the written and spoken word, and usually has an extensive vocabulary with a flair for languages.

As an adolescent, the Pig lady will be extremely sensitive. A creative outlet is vital for her and she will strive for approval. She will love to be around others. Any tendency to go to extremes should be observed and sound guidance and wisdom given. Encourage her to speak of her feelings and to maintain a healthy life.

PIG WOMAN AND CAREER

The Pig woman is one of the most creative of the animal signs! She has a powerful drive and a natural enthusiasm, which produce a dynamic personality. She is also very much affected by her emotions, and this factor can prevent her from succeeding in her vocations. This is unfortunate as she has so much to offer.

The Pig woman's work environment needs to focus on an expression of herself. Therefore mundane work seldom suits her, as she cannot put her emotions into it. Personalized fields such as writing, poetry, and higher education would best suit her for this reason. She should avoid getting stuck in mundane work and always look for a creative outlet. The Pig lady can also make a wonderful counselor and teacher in her mature years.

Good career choices include artist, writer, psychologist, therapist, child counselor, photographer, herbalist, feng shui advisor, legal expert, and social worker. She would also probably be fulfilled in accounting and banking positions as she naturally pays attention to detail.

PIG WOMAN IN THE TWENTY-FIRST CENTURY

The Pig woman believes in solid, down-to-earth values. As we enter the twenty-first century, her excellent practical energy can be of great benefit to the society of which she is part.

The Pig woman has a special connection to children and youth in general. Her love life can sometimes be turbulent in the next few years, as she learns to adapt to a rapidly changing world where her faith in her belief system will be tested. She will emerge victorious in spite this, however.

The Pig woman should do all she can to develop herself. She should concentrate on courses to encourage her creativity and assertiveness to promote self-acceptance and personal development, both very important issues for most Pig ladies.

The twenty-first century will be an intensely maturing time for the Pig woman. Her practical strength will probably find her taking on the role of personal Rock of Gibraltar for many of her associates and learning to become more of the wise mother figure she is destined to be.

PIG WOMAN AND SPIRITUALITY

The Pig woman has very intense and profound values. She relates to healing and nurturing others in a sincere way. Her spiritual life is usually quite defined. Some Pig ladies love to follow specific rituals or exercises in their work.

She intuitively relates well to the profound goddess mothers of Isis and Demeter, whose nurturing qualities were worshipped for centuries. Other Pig ladies relate to the shamanism or natural earth healing and animal wisdom.

The Pig woman has her feet firmly on the ground. Hence, any spiritual work that she undertakes must be connected to her life and have solid meaning to it for her to fully embrace it in any powerful way. Having a grounded spiritual life actually helps her avoid overindulgence and escape.

As the Pig lady loves to mother, she is one of the animal signs that works well as a co-coordinator of a group of devotees (as long as she watches her desire to take total control!). In practicing her own rituals, the Pig woman should do so in an outside setting. Her spirit flies free in the beauty of nature.

RITUAL WORK FOR THE PIG WOMAN

INVOKING ISIS FOR HEALING AND REQUESTS

Ritual Tools

· Hand of Fatima (may be purchased at magick or jewelry shops)
· A vase full of fresh-cut pink and purple flowers (pick them yourself, if possible)
· A handful of any of the following: rose petals, lavender flowers, frankincense
· One stick each of rose and frankincense incense
· One violet and one pink candle
· A piece of silver jewelry
· Ritual robes in the colors of deep blue or pink

Ritual Time

Waxing to full moon in Taurus or Libra.

Dress in your robes and prepare your altar with the above magickal tools, preferably outside in the light of the moon. Light the candles and incense. Take the charm and the jewelry in both hands as an offering for the goddess Isis. Meditate on the power of the goddess to heal and create miracles.

Invoke the goddess by chanting the following:

"Isis, I invoke your powerful healing energies in my everyday life. As you stood for the eternal feminine power of the mother, may my nurturing energy respect the power it has to heal or destroy. I petition you for the following success: [*state your request here*]. May your divine blessing and protection surround me."

Allow the candles and incense to burn for at least an hour. Then snuff out the candles. Make a permanent altar in your home dedicated to the Great Mother. Wear the charm in her memory and honor to help you weave her magick.

INVOKING FORTUNA FOR LOVE

Ritual Tools

· A small cornucopia or a picture of one to represent sexuality and power
· An apple, cut in half at time of ritual
· Two red candles and two pink candles
· One stick each of rose and lavender incense for balance in love and mind
· One rose quartz crystal
· Two handfuls of rose petals, dried or fresh
· A glass of red wine or cider
· A piece of ginger root for increased sexual power
· A piece of myrrh incense for healing properties
· Ylang-ylang and rose oils or incense
· Pink ritual robe

Ritual Time

Full moon in Taurus or Libra.

Prior to the ritual, bathe in the essential oils. If you don't have a bath, burn the incense while you refresh or wash yourself. Dress in your robe and prepare the altar with the magickal tools. Stand in front of the altar and take the cornucopia in hand. Light the candles and incense and invoke the goddess Fortuna by chanting the following:

> "Goddess of plenty, bring good fortune to me in my love life [*if single*]. I realize the need for a partner in my life and believe I have the power to attract the right one. [*If you are in a loving union already, ask the goddess to bless your union and protect it.*] I honor the Goddess and do not seek control over my mate but request a respectful and loving partner. [*To clear yourself of an unsatisfactory relationship, request the goddess to 'move me on to another relationship reflecting good fortune.'*]"

Conclude your ritual by scattering the rose petals over your altar space, snuffing out the candles, and raising a glass of wine or cider in honor of the goddess.

Take the seeds of the apple and scatter them over your altar to dry. Then place them under your bed, or you may like to create a small sachet bag in pink material. Place the seeds, rose petals, the cornucopia, and the rose quartz in it and carry it with you in your handbag or dress. You may also choose to leave it on the altar space in honor of the goddess.

MEDITATION FOR CALM AND FOCUSING

After taking a long bath or shower, lie down in a comfortable place. If it is a nice day, practice your meditation exercise outside under a tree or near a quiet spot. Otherwise, close your eyes and visualize yourself lying on soft, lush grass in a wide, open field.

Take three deep, slow breaths in and out. Visualize your body against the earth. Feel the earth's warmth, its impenetrable strength beneath you, and the power of its ageless wisdom.

Release your thoughts now and delve deep down into the earth. You are channeling with a brilliant white light, swirling through millions of years of earth and rock, down, down into the deep, dark earth. Plummeting further and further, crashing through stones, you find yourself in the middle of the earth!

Imagine this center. You are creating whatever you like: a secret tropical garden, a rock pool so deep you think it will never end, a golden mansion or a house perched on a hill. Explore this world you have created and take whatever refuge you wish: swim in the pool, open the doors of the mansion, or smell all the wonderful flowers of the lush, tropical garden.

When you have taken enough time, see your thoughts connected to that body still lying on the earth above. A string is linked to you and suddenly you feel a tug in your chest to go back to it. In a swift moment you are being pulled timelessly and effortlessly back up toward that body. In an instant you are back inside your body and you feel the grass again under you.

Now you are looking at the sky and all the trees and the huge sun above. You feel your spirit rising above your body and you are flying up toward the sky. You fly toward the tree branches high above you and you are turning and sweeping amongst all the leaves and tall trees. You're flying with the birds and bees, and you feel like a part of all that surrounds you. You are separate yet connected, and

your mind is free of all tension and stress. You are dancing effortlessly and grace-
fully in the air.

You turn now and again and see that thin thread that links you to that body
lying on the grass. Look down on that body and see it, see your dress and your figure. Be kind to your body. It serves you well for the purpose it has. When you have
had enough time flying in the air, you feel a tug and again feel yourself being
drawn effortlessly back toward that body. Again you are now in your body and
feeling the earth beneath it.

Take three deep breaths and breathe out slowly. When you open your eyes you
feel at peace and connected to everything around you. You feel refreshed and confident to direct your body to fulfill your dreams.

Ox Woman

THE NATURAL EMPRESS

CHARMS AND SYMBOLS

Tarot card:	The Empress, which represents feminine empowerment
Moon phase:	Waxing to full
Celestial bodies:	Jupiter
Herbs and plants:	Vervain, clove, endive
Colors:	Browns, earth shades, blues, greens
Crystals and gemstones:	Agate, emerald, jade
Incense:	Honeysuckle, sage
Lucky day:	Friday
Lucky numbers:	3, 12, 21
Ritual colors:	Blue, camel, white
Ritual robes:	Wool, natural fibers, cotton
Magickal symbols:	Oxen or bulls, horns, wreaths, rosaries, mirrors, pomegranates, crowns, diadems
Goddesses:	The nurturer, the Mother Earth (associated with the bovine), the provider
Theme song:	"That's All Right" by Elvis Presley

ASSOCIATED GODDESSES FOR THE OX WOMAN

Hathor: Egyptian goddess of the sky, Hathor was the symbolic mother of the pharaohs. Her father was the sun god. Hathor is associated with the great mother and nurturer concept. She is portrayed holding the ankh, symbol of the life force energy. She is often depicted as a winged cow and, in some mythology, portrayed as giving birth to the universe.

Frigg: Nordic goddess of the earth mother energy. She was associated with childbirth, motherhood, and sexuality. She was also thought of as the goddess of marriage. Frigg's symbols were the sword and keys, and in mythology she is said to have sat beside the god Odin at his throne.

Kunapipi: Mother goddess of the Aboriginal Australians.

Hera: Greek goddess of motherhood. Wife to Zeus known for her revengeful power when crossed. Her animals were the cow and the peacock.

POSITIVE TRAITS

earth mother	matriarchal
enduring	creative
nurturing	protective
loving	strong-willed
persistent	genuine
organized	Olympic strength
loyal	honorable

NEGATIVE TRAITS

domineering	staid
rigid	immovable
exacting	overpowering
workaholic	demanding
unimaginative	too trusting
controlling	melancholic
naive	competitive

FAMOUS OX WOMEN

Hedy Lamarr · Meryl Streep · Enya · Vivien Leigh · Heather Locklear
Meg Ryan · Catherine Freeman · Princess Diana · Margaret Thatcher
Sigourney Weaver · Jane Fonda · Juliette Lewis · Neve Campbell

OX WOMAN'S NUMBER

1 You will forge new pathways in life and are well-suited to public service. You need to take on leading roles with responsibilities as your energy drive is very high.

2 You are a gentle and caring Ox, and need a strong partner. Beware you don't fall victim to being relied on too much. Your natural caring qualities are increased under this number.

3 Ms. Communicator Ox. You are destined to carry loads for others. You may be a political commentator or human rights journalist or an important public service figure.

4 Ms. Steadfast Ox, the true Rock of Gibraltar. People will rely on you to help them in times of need. A great counselor and naturally supportive, you set high standards for yourself and others.

5 You will be a bit more relaxed than other Oxen and will tend to need room to express yourself. You suit dynamic, active fields of work.

6 Ms. Loving Ox, you are a natural wife and mother. You will probably be known in your circle as a major matriarchal figure and will be sought as an advisor.

7 Intuitive Ox. You are sensitive, and need to watch depression and loneliness as well as an inclination to take life a little too seriously. Adopt a sense of fair play and take notice of your psychic flashes. You are a creative little Ox!

8 Ox with lots of energy, you have very strong likes and dislikes. You have the drive to run an empire, or at least your own company. Watch rigidity and overwork, energetic Ox!

9 An excellent teaching Ox and advisor. You have a penetrating mind and may be attracted to government or institutional endeavors.

THE EMPRESS!

Professional, hard-working, and characteristically self-effacing, the Ox woman successfully encapsulates the trait of the true empress: she is born to rule through her spiritual connection to the immense nurturing power of the goddesses she is allied with.

The Ox woman is pure female power and strength. Catherine Freeman, Olympic gold medallist and international sports figure, is born under the sign of the Ox. Her drive, determination, and dedication to win in a highly competitive athletic field after many obstacles in her youth epitomizes the formidable qualities of women born under this sign. Catherine is an extraordinary role model and an inspirational figure.

Another unforgettable Ox lady is the legendary actress Vivien Leigh. She sailed across the sea to win an acting role that was sought out by all the actresses of the time. Her determination to seize the role and then to give her all portraying Scarlett O'Hara in the exceptionally successful movie *Gone with the Wind* required immense physical and psychological stamina. Reportedly, Vivien fought quite a battle to play Scarlett as the strong-willed and indomitable figure that she was. Her performance and staying power in the marathon-length production, which was fraught with financial problems and stress, earned her an Academy Award and permanent status as a movie goddess. Vivien possessed, like all her Ox woman sisters do today, an ox-type determination and amazing persistence to achieve her ambition.

Passionate, loyal, and forbearing, the Ox woman draws on her incredible energy reserves to provide for and nurture all around her. In her intrinsic strength, she may forget that her own mortal body needs caring for too.

The Ox woman may overuse her strength and forget to allow others to pull their weight. She must remember that others may not be as loyal as she and they can take advantage of her personal strength. Conversely, she may also demand too much in return, not realizing that not all people have the same staying power that she has been given.

Like all women associated with the Earth Goddess, the Ox woman must balance her power with the wisdom of the true Earth Mother. Learning to let go and watch others progress in their lives without her presence or assistance is an important lesson for the Ox lady.

The Ox woman faces challenges in areas of overwork, over-responsibility, and rigidity. She often forgets to ask for help or appears so powerful that she does not seem to need it, leaving her feeling alone when there is usually a helping hand waiting to be called upon. In other cases, she asks so much of herself that she is frequently disappointed. The Ox woman has high standards to which she subjects herself and others. She perceives that others have let her down when she has needed their help, when in fact they have just not been able to meet the high standards that she expects of them.

As dedicated as she is, and this is an admirable quality, the Ox lady needs to lighten up and try to release herself to the energies available from the magickal and playful goddesses. Melancholy, depression, and irritability can result if she does not feel appreciated and becomes too intense with the people around her. She needs to refrain from pushing herself and others beyond their limits. Life wasn't meant to be all hard work, Lady Ox!

The Ox woman is a fabulous organizer and administrator. She can be an invaluable asset to any person or group who needs her Olympic strength to get things done. No one can claim the Ox lady doesn't do her fair share!

Life usually places the Ox woman in situations where she is tested to the limits and where she feels that a tremendous burden lies with her. If she remembers her sacred affiliation to the Earth Goddess energy she will reach a new level of balance. She must learn to respect her power as a nurturer, a provider, and potentially a healer, while at the same time acknowledging that she sometimes pushes herself over the limit in order to prove herself.

Like the famous Greek goddess and ruler, Hera, wife to the Greek god Zeus, the Ox woman gets very angry if she is not treated with the respect she knows she deserves. She can internalize this anger, which can lead to emotional and physical illness. The Ox woman must learn to be more self-giving, and know when it is time to withdraw her energies back to herself to replenish her own body and spirit. As the goddess gives, so she can take her sovereignty back, thus giving her a more wise and temperate outlook.

It is also paramount for the Ox woman to stand back and see what she has truly accomplished in her life. She is far too critical of herself and expends too much energy trying to achieve ideals that will not come to fruition in the real world. One of the utmost challenges for the Ox woman is to stop being too demanding of herself and too fixed in her expectations of what she should be doing and accomplishing.

The late Princess Diana, born under the sign of the metal Ox, displayed the powerful nurturing characteristics of the Ox woman in her care for people around the world. When she declared that she wanted to be the "Queen of Hearts," Diana had already reached her ambition. She may never have been crowned queen, but she was an Empress in the eyes of many people.

The flipside to Diana's kindness and concern for others was her self-criticism. This was fanned by traits of perfectionism and melancholy that were manifested in her anger toward the position she had found herself in. She internalized this anger, which punished her for not living up to the ideal put upon her, both by the people around her and by herself. She suffered emotional illness until she was able to free her emotions and let go of some of her demands on herself. Diana had to learn to forgive and move on, though this may have taken more personal resilience than she realized she had.

For all the difficulties in her life, Diana expressed the true spirit of the Earth Goddess in her tireless work for charity and those with whom she felt empathy. She achieved true success and goddesslike status, which was made all the more remarkable by the obstacles she overcame.

OX WOMAN AND LOVE

The Ox woman has a powerful love nature: passionate, intense, and profound, yet at the same time capable of ravaging anger and hurt. She loves and, indeed, hates with an equal intensity. Vivien Leigh, a Scorpio Ox, was passionately attracted to Goat man Laurence Olivier to the point of leaving her husband and young daughter to be with him. Yet this union ended when Laurence found another partner, and Vivien remained in love with him.

No other animal sign (with the exception of perhaps the Tiger lady) has the same incredible store of energy the Ox woman devotes, and at times sacrifices, to her love object.

The Ox woman's endless vitality and sexual energy makes her a dedicated partner for any mate. But, to refer to Hera again, her love can turn to violence if her lover does not respect her. Hence, the potential mate of any Ox woman should

Ox Woman and Compatibility

Ox & Rat
♡♡
Rat is fun; Ox is stable and nurturing. Can work if Rat is mature and loyal.

Ox & Ox
♡♡♡♡
Yes! They will sustain and help each other. Both of them deeply value and appreciate family.

Ox & Tiger
♡♡
Ox gives the nurturing Tiger what the Tiger needs, but power struggles are likely.

Ox & Cat
♡♡♡
These two can have quite a productive relationship if they share mutual interests.

Ox & Dragon
♡♡♡
Dragon loves Ox's strength, but may be too changeable for firm Ox.

Ox & Snake
♡
Ox must beware of jealousy and uneven passions here. Snake will ignite the sexual fires though!

Ox & Horse
♡♡♡
Good. Horse needs discipline and Ox will take Horse on.

Ox & Goat
♡♡
Ox has the fortitude, Goat the sensitivity. Ox needs to learn not to overpower though.

Ox & Monkey
♡♡♡
Clever Monkey finds a stable home and lots of security. Ox appreciates the entertainment.

Ox & Rooster
♡♡♡
This can work out well as Rooster finds Ox to be a good audience.

Ox & Dog
♡♡♡
Loyal, faithful relationship where both have shared ideals.

Ox & Pig
♡♡♡♡
A great partnership of like minds and hearts. Both value the hearth and home.

♡♡♡♡ = excellent   ♡♡♡ = good   ♡♡ = fair   ♡ = difficult

bear this in mind and treat and revere her as an equal. Partners should not make the mistake of viewing her as just the gracious, patient mother figure that she is. Prince Charles did not see the complexity of his wife, Ox woman Princess Diana. He was to learn that she held many other sides to her personality that would not lie dormant.

There is a peculiar paradox in the Ox woman: she will command and win respect from her coworkers, yet she is willing to take second-best treatment from her mate. This, in turn, leads to frustration, which may well be hidden for long periods of time. But eventually it will surface to play out well-fuelled revenge!

Drawing from an analogy with the Empress in the tarot, the Ox woman must heed emotional sovereignty. That is, she must recognize the power of her love force and take refuge in it when she needs to. It is she who has the control within; it is not dependent on another person's approval and attention.

The tarot's Empress esoterically symbolizes the bounty of Mother Earth's graciousness and the earth energy that sustains us all. The Ox woman needs to defer to this power that is linked to her and nourish her innate spirit in order to advance as an individual. The depth of Mother Earth's power also shows in her unbridled passionate nature, which can sweep her and all those around her along in a whirlwind trip. Yet the Ox woman's family and friends will often feel her healing energy. The Ox lady can be a very affectionate and caring wife and mother.

Ox woman mothers tend to give their children a prevailing aura of love and security, which can be a little overpowering at times. She is wise to instill in her children a sense of autonomy and encourage self-reliance, as she tends to be too giving and generous of spirit. This can lead to self-exhaustion and overdependence from her offspring.

As she is also subject to intense feelings, the Ox woman must also be careful not to subject herself to guilt-ridden episodes following times when she has sought too much passion from her partner. The Ox woman finds her focused mind usually has two objectives: her children and her partner. She may find it difficult to balance the two in this respect, and may experience unnecessary feelings of guilt toward one or the other.

It is imperative for the Ox lady to remain grounded in herself, and allocate time to find balance in her life. She must learn to assert her own feminine needs, and displace the anger and resentment that may build up if she fails to focus on herself more often.

At heart, the Ox woman seeks a potent, centered mate who will live at peace with her and admire her strength.

OX WOMAN AND HEALTH

The Ox woman's health is normally excellent as she has almost Olympic strength! She must be aware of nervous or mental exhaustion or fatigue however, as she tends to always push herself to her limits. Blessed with such a powerful physique, she has the potential to live to be old if she takes care of her diet, follows checkups, and gets sufficient rest. Regular workouts or strenuous exercise can help her burn off the effects of too much stress.

OX WOMAN AND FINANCES

The Ox woman is normally a very industrious worker, so she naturally accumulates security over her life. She is prudent and a clever investor who enjoys watching her savings grow. Disciplined and precise, she will study the best methods of increasing her investments. Her lucky financial areas involve real estate and safe government bonds. She will not be attracted to risky ventures and has a good nose for a bargain.

OX WOMAN AS A CHILD

The Ox child is generally serious, principled, and possesses very strong ideas. Firm in her convictions, she loves to be the focus of leadership in her circle. She will take on a mothering role way beyond her years to any young child that plays with her—and even the stray adult too, if you let her!

Sometimes prone to temper swings if not allowed her own way, the Ox child has a nature that holds out for what she wants and generally won't give in till she has it! Innately idealistic, she needs to be taught how her inner convictions can make real achievements possible in the real world.

The Ox child needs much security and encouragement for her goals in her life, or she tends to fall subject to nervous tension and exhaustion and concurrent problems. She should be given support to pursue a career that uses her sincerity of thought.

Little Miss Ox can be quite athletic and may need plenty of time for exercise and stimulating activities. She may even like to play rough with the boys in a game of baseball. Again, she will most likely show them who's boss, which may lead to boisterous pursuits and even the occasional scuffle! However, Miss Ox is much more sensitive than she will usually appear.

OX WOMAN AND CAREER

The Ox woman finds happiness in using her strength to nurture others. She would therefore usually do well in physically demanding careers that require long hours or much physical and mental effort. She naturally exerts energy and would do well in a group environment. So long as her efforts are noticed, the Ox lady will take on any job. She works well with others.

Good career choices for the Ox woman include physical education teacher, social worker, psychologist, counselor, nurse and other medical positions, and team-oriented jobs such as sport coach, trainer, activity organizer, or co-coordinator and motivational speaker. The Ox woman also has a marvellous creative side, and could adapt herself to acting or thespian roles.

Producing and playing music can also be suited professions. Ox woman Enya serenades the world's spirit with her inspirational and ethereal music. In a typical Earth Goddess way, she heals and soothes us.

The Ox woman's organizational abilities can find expression in politics and government positions. She is not, however, suited to purely financial work, or jobs that do not involve effort and personal or team spirit.

OX WOMAN IN THE TWENTY-FIRST CENTURY

In the new time and century, the Ox woman will be formidable, as she has great power to make things happen. Her zeal and drive make her a natural reformer and head of welfare organizations. She needs to contribute to her community and will naturally gravitate to positions of leadership and innovation. Her main challenge is to believe in her capacity to contribute as she sometimes lacks confidence in herself.

OX WOMAN AND SPIRITUALITY

The feminine principles of goddess energy and worship are important for the Ox woman to get in touch with. Acceptance of her divine power and realization of her connection to the Earth Mother can alleviate this woman's suffering as she travels through her journey. As the Ox woman relates so much to the sacred gifts of the earth, she also connects to the full moon energy of the Egyptian goddess Hathor and the Nordic goddess Frigg. The legends and energies of the Earth Goddesses should be studied by the Ox woman in her search for her own sacred self, as it will affirm her commitments as well as give her a sense of self-worth.

RITUAL WORK FOR THE OX WOMAN

INVOKING HATHOR FOR SPECIAL PETITIONS

Ritual Tools
· A small glass of red wine (in a crystal goblet, if possible)
· A vase full of red and yellow flowers
· A citrine crystal and a garnet
· One musical instrument or a picture of one
· One stick each of frankincense and benzoin incense
· Joyous music to play later (CD)

Ritual Time
Full moon period.

Prepare your altar with the above magickal tools. Light the candles and incense. Invoke the goddess by softly chanting the following:

> "Hathor, powerful mother goddess of the sky, give me the strength to achieve my goals [*state goals here*]. I believe in your divinity as expressed in your power and aura. Help me be empowered by my strengths, but also to moderate them. You are the Wild Ox, you are the Great Mother spirit within me. I hold your sacred energy and truth. I honor your magick."

Visualize a great sky around you. See the goddess energy in spiritual form as a light filling the sky space. Anoint your head (at the third-eye point just between your eyebrows) with a drop of the red wine.

Recite to yourself:

> "I honor the lifeblood of the goddess and I acknowledge this life force in all people. I do not seek to control others but only to enhance their spirit. I believe in the power of my sacred self and my potential to overcome physical obstacles with my spirit. I refuse to be downtrodden or oppressed. I honor and identify with my sacred Ox energy."

Conclude the ritual by grounding yourself with the energy of the crystals. Hold one each in the palms of your hands. Play some joyous music, have a dance with the goddess, and toast her with the red wine.

INVOKING FRIGG FOR LOVE

Ritual Tools
· A small posy of wildflowers (best picked by your own hand)
· A mixture of twenty-four red and pink beads threaded on a red cotton string
· One stick each of pine and sandalwood incense
· Two red candles
· Your ritual robe of either wool or cotton in greens or blues
· A piece of red material
· A shiny new key in honor of the goddess

Ritual Time
Full moon in Taurus.

Set up your altar with the items listed above. Dress in your robes and light the candles and incense. Invoke the goddess Frigg by chanting the following verse:

> "Great goddess of fertility and childbirth, I invoke your divine power. I seek a worthy partner to share my magick and power with. Help me to realize my limitations while always allowing me to see the stars. I invoke your help in drawing to me the partner my soul desires and needs."

Dedicate the flowers and beads to Frigg. Wrap the beads in the red material and place it somewhere close to where you retire. Before you sleep at night, visualize your partner coming into your life. Alternatively, carry the beads with you to remind you of the power you have within to find happiness. After the conclusion of the ceremony, snuff out the candles and the incense.

MEDITATION FOR CALM AND FOCUSING

Relax in your favorite position and close your eyes. See yourself standing in the middle of a verdant field surrounded by the beauty of nature. You can feel the gentle breeze against your face and hear the song of birds. Within yourself you feel secure and content. It seems as if Mother Earth herself is your hostess.

A tall, imposing woman approaches you. She has a kind, nurturing expression, as well as a quiet dignity. She is dressed in cream cotton robes with a brown belt around her waist. You know intuitively she is your inner goddess. In her right hand she carries a shining gold key. In her left hand she carries a floral crown made of white roses.

She looks deeply into your eyes and motions you to stand. You follow this request and stand before her. She places the floral crown on your head and the key in your hands. She bends close to you and says, "Follow your destiny, child of earth. The key symbolizes your freedom and the crown symbolizes your many strengths."

You feel the love coming from her to you. You feel strong and at one with all life. After a moment, you look around and see you are in a circle of dear animal familiars (cherished pets you have loved or love now). You can see their kind, gentle eyes looking right at you. Serene and free, you rejoice in their attendance. You are amongst friends, yet you are also a leader.

Laughing, you take off the floral crown and break up the petals. You scatter them all around your circle of love. This symbolizes your inner power to give as you choose without fear of loss. Taking the key, you place it carefully in the center of your circle. You leave it there with your loved ones as a symbol of freedom in your spiritual domain. Your inner goddess smiles to see your play. You feel she supports you in everything you do.

Come out of your meditation and take a moment to thank Mother Earth for her bounty in the form of animals and nature. Also thank your special goddess. Return to this place whenever you feel you need to nurture or heal yourself.

PART IV

Warrior Goddess Women

Horse Woman

THE NATURAL WARRIOR

CHARMS AND SYMBOLS

Tarot card:	Strength, which represents the taming of the inner beast
Moon phase:	Waxing to full
Celestial bodies:	Sun
Herbs and plants:	Marigold, pineapple, peony
Colors:	Gold, yellow, earth tones
Crystals and gemstones:	Amber, citrine quartz
Incense:	Witch hazel, sandalwood, frankincense
Lucky day:	Sunday
Lucky numbers:	1, 10
Ritual colors:	Yellows, oranges
Ritual robes:	Free-flowing garments, cottons
Magickal symbols:	Horses, horseshoes, unicorns
Goddesses:	The leaders, maiden warriors
Theme song:	"Born to Run" by Bruce Springsteen

ASSOCIATED GODDESSES FOR THE HORSE WOMAN

Epona: Horse goddess of the ancient Gauls, Epona represents bravery, freedom, and courage, and was taken to heart by the Romans. She is usually shown riding a horse carrying fruit or corn. Epona is believed to guide the soul on its final journey to the afterworld. The kings of Ireland were associated symbolically with the white mare (as a representation of rebirth) and it is believed this came from the cult of Epona that existed throughout Spain, Italy, and Britain.

Brigantia: A Celtic goddess of war and a patron of the arts. Often portrayed wearing a helmet and carrying a trident, Brigantia symbolizes victory, energy, and celebration. This goddess became known as Saint Brigit in Ireland, and a cult of priestesses was dedicated to her. She was a teacher of the martial arts, and her soldiers were known as "brigands."

Morrigan: A Celtic goddess who was associated with war and the battlefield, Morrigan was strongly linked to horses and could change shape into an animal at will. She was also known as the crone Macha, Great Queen of the Phantoms.

Lady Godiva: This title is translated as "Lady Goddess." *Goda* is the Nordic name for Freya, while *diva* is the Indo-European word for "goddess." Lady Godiva was said to ride naked on horseback to symbolize rebirth and fertility.

POSITIVE TRAITS

dynamic	passionate
vivacious	vital
risk-taker	initiator
quick	honest
energetic	active
headstrong	leader
gutsy	autonomous
decisive	independent
bold	versatile
idealistic	unbridled

NEGATIVE TRAITS

materialistic	demanding
noncommittal	scattered
impulsive	domineering
flighty	gambler
impatient	nonreflective
naive	impatient
bossy	selfish
aloof	inconsiderate
overpowering	superficial
isolated	indifferent

fAMOUS HORSE WOMEN

Helena Bonham Carter · Halle Berry · Téa Leoni
Rita Hayworth · Cindy Crawford · Cherie Blair · Barbra Streisand
Robin Wright Penn · Joanne Woodward · Jacqueline Susann
Aretha Franklin · Princess Margaret · Ellen Barkin

HORSE WOMAN'S NUMBER

1 You have the capacity to lead your own army—or at least your own fan club! Dynamic and forceful, you are a true battle Horse!

2 Gentle and peaceful, you require a Horse mate and a nice stable.

3 You have the gift of gab, Mrs. Ed, and are a great entertainer. You need plenty of stimulation and challenges.

4 You can be a great source of direction to others and lead very effectively. Watch rigidity though.

5 As the actress Horse, you have the marvelous capacity to turn your dreams into realities—but don't get lost in them.

6 Peacemaker and lover, you can be extremely altruistic for a Horse.

7 Horse with a sixth sense. You are very intuitive and need creative pursuits.

8 Tough Horse lady! You can drive a bargain and stick to one. Practice moderation.

9 As a dynamic partying Horse, you need free rein and plenty of paddock to roam in!

THE WARRIOR!

The Horse woman is a powerful and formidable energy. The goddess Epona, traditionally associated with the horse, epitomizes the Horse woman's ability to surmount obstacles and free herself from restrictions. Freedom-loving, passionate, and strong, the Horse woman is a dynamic worker who is capable of attaining larger-than-life goals.

The Horse woman is full of high ideals, and often takes up one cause or another in order to release the champion within. At the same time, there is a part of her that is elusive and free-spirited—almost unattainable. These characteristics make her a complex and fascinating person.

Horse woman Barbra Streisand first flashed on the screen as the title character in *Funny Girl,* a role that showed off her great vitality. Later as a producer, director, and creative power, she fully showed herself to be the warrior, enduring and powerful enough to retain her appeal through several generations.

Horse lady Jacqueline Susann rewrote the way women viewed themselves with her liberated novels, which expressed the raw passion and sexuality of this sign. Rita Hayworth expressed her dynamic Horse power on the big screen.

The Horse woman gallops toward her life's convictions and works like a horse to carry them out. Her belief in herself is a powerful charisma that, though arresting, is also charmingly fresh and uplifting.

As she has an inordinate amount of physical and inner strength, the Horse woman often takes on her plough role and can be a workaholic. She needs to roam the pastures every now and then to simply relax and replenish her resources. Whether this is taking a break somewhere or concentrating on a hobby that she enjoys does not matter as long as it is not connected to her usual work.

The Horse woman's desire to get things done occasionally makes her more than a little impatient with those around her who do not have her energy. She does at a gallop what others may do just at a canter. This may cause her to be bossy and a touch overbearing, which she needs to keep in check. On the other hand, this type of intensity can be beneficial if she is leading a group or project that needs a boost of her vital energy to keep it moving.

The Horse lady is not a natural leader like her Rat or Dragon sisters, however her inherent strength can often place her in such a role. Though she may not deliberately seek a pivotal part, she often finds herself in one and will inject powerful energy into anything she undertakes.

Those around the Horse woman may be carried away with her exuberance and aura of strength. They may also unintentionally expect more of her than she is able to give. But they will feel energized by her natural sense of movement and love of freedom. Ironically, it is the Horse lady's inherent need to move and be free that can often lead her away from the vital support her friends and family provide.

Headstrong, bold, and somewhat of a risk-taker, the Horse lady needs to realize that a little self-reflection will help her find even more power. Like her token animal, she must tame her animal instincts to realize her greatest achievements.

She must also realize that no matter how great her own energy, it is important to understand the value of others' contributions, particularly in the many causes she supports; she does not really have to carry the load all by herself. Wisdom will teach the Horse appreciation of group and team efforts.

Her considerable reserves of power and strength, in addition to her true dedication to life, makes her an outward-thinking and highly animated animal sign. Her challenges, therefore, lie in the realm of careful reflection and in learning to develop her intuition. Honest and largely straightforward, the Horse woman sometimes misses out on the more subtle undercurrents of life.

Like the warrior goddesses she relates to, the Horse lady is ever ready to engage in the battle of life. Yet sometimes she is defeated by life's dirty politics. This is a pity because the Horse lady has a brave and idealistic heart and usually good self-esteem.

A sensual, earthy sign, the Horse lady can be demandingly creative. This Goddess Sign needs to practice temperance and relaxation in her paddock or she will burn herself out. She must also be careful of experimenting with artificial substances and seeking the illusions of freedom through drugs and other intoxicants. She should seek the natural highs abundantly available to her in the natural world.

The Horse woman needs to watch that she is not too concerned with materialism and ambition and remember to keep her spiritual ideals alive. Her desire to succeed can interfere with the gentler aspects of love and family and leave her discontented. However, as she matures as a soul, the Horse lady learns to listen to the wisdom of those who have experienced other facets of life.

Before this happens, the Horse lady may run in where angels fear to tread. She can be self-absorbed in her drive to achieve, and will fight being placed in a sub-ordinate position. On the plus side, the Horse lady has a strong will to achieve. If focused, she can make an enormous difference in the world around her.

HORSE WOMAN AND LOVE

Audacious, bright, and sexy, the Horse lady takes hearts like hostages. She loves her freedom, but will still seek a natural companion in life. She will determinedly seek her soul mate, and will give this mate her strength and protection.

The Horse lady desires a gentle and emotional partner. She is not suited to thrill-seekers or overly ambitious mates unless their ambitions are strongly aligned. She is tender-hearted and more sentimental then she appears to be, and often prepared to risk everything for love.

Sometimes naive and impulsive when young, the Horse lady really needs to develop her maturity before successfully settling down. She loves to play the field, however! Barbra Streisand and Cindy Crawford represent Horse ladies who have needed to mature and evolve before finding their true loves.

Her passion and vitality naturally lead her to settle down early, but this will only work if she has been fortunate enough to meet her right partner. Once she is happy, the Horse lady is devoted and seldom strays unless she is truly miserable. Joanne Woodward found her great love with actor Paul Newman.

If the Horse woman does not settle when young, she will roam free for quite a while in her idealistic search for the freedom fighter she can identify with. She will never allow herself to be fenced in and will strive toward her own sense of individuality. She has no difficulty in drawing partners to her side as her innate sex appeal and energy is powerful, but she may need to examine her mate's capac-ity to give her freedom. A good relationship for the Horse woman is one that moves with her while at the same time giving her security.

The Horse lady's needs in a partnership are shared values, romance, and gen-uine sensitivity. The right mate will support her passions and, ideally, share them, or at least hold great respect for them. She also needs a gentle partner. In return, the Horse lady will truly honor her mate and will prove a fabulous support to her partner so long as she pulls in the reins on her own ambitions.

Horse Woman and Compatibility

Horse & Rat
♡

Forget it. Rat is not Horse lady's gentle ideal! Both have to lead.

Horse & Ox
♡♡♡

Good. These two hold mutual respect to be a necessity in love.

Horse & Tiger
♡♡♡

This match can work if Tiger can be tamed. The ground rules must be established early though.

Horse & Cat
♡

Difficult, but Cat has the gentle side Horse seeks. Privacy is important.

Horse & Dragon
♡♡

Strong pair if both stay tolerant of each other's demands and needs.

Horse & Snake
♡

Difficult as Snake will have too many other distractions.

Horse & Horse
♡♡♡♡

Great empathy between minds of like passions. Excellent mates!

Horse & Goat
♡♡♡

A potentially well-rounded relationship here. Goat has artist's qualities that Horse will gravitate toward.

Horse & Monkey
♡

No. Monkey usually won't settle with solid Horse.

Horse & Rooster
♡♡

Roosters are usually into their ego too much, which will leave little room to nurture Horse's needs.

Horse & Dog
♡♡

Good potential if both are family-oriented and ready to settle down.

Horse & Pig
♡♡

These two loyal signs will make a go of it, but need commonality to last.

♡♡♡♡ – excellent   ♡♡♡ = good   ♡♡ = fair   ♡ = difficult

As a mother, the Horse lady is also devoted, but unruly foals will test her patience, as she is not one to suffer disobedience. She has a quick temper, and given her dominant tendency, can have regimental ideas of upbringing. Her capacity to organize is wonderful, but she needs to relax and chill out when trying to keep her children in line. She will have more success if she just lets them act up as all children do from time to time.

HORSE WOMAN AND HEALTH

This sign can really be said to be as strong as a horse. There is meaning here for the Horse lady as she usually has the blessing of a particularly healthy constitution and athletic ability. However, she does not take enough time to relax, and should avoid overstraining her reserve or she will become a beast of burden to herself.

Dancing, relaxation, swimming, and walking are beneficial pursuits, as is a healthy diet full of leafy vegetables and fruits. She should avoid excessive carbohydrates and caffeine that she tends to indulge in to keep her moving. Meditation, regular exercise, and medical check-ups are important to maintain her natural vitality levels.

Overwork and overdoing it in her personal life are two distinct danger areas the Horse lady should be aware of. Her vulnerable areas are her back, skeleton, and breasts. She needs to watch accidents caused through carelessness.

HORSE WOMAN AND FINANCES

This hard worker usually manages to save and is often cunning with her investments. She has a natural achieving energy that generally inspires her to be very astute and careful with her funds. However, she must beware of get-rich schemes that she may be introduced to by well-meaning associates who don't have the same cunning as the Horse lady but may influence her all the same. Rather than take on schemes that she has not properly thought through, the Horse lady is wise to make her own thorough choices and resist others' influence as a general rule.

HORSE WOMAN AS A CHILD

This little Filly loves to be just that: a playful and carefree child that has no fear and no hesitation to jump fences. She loves myth, romance, and legend.

She may show athletic and physical education talents, which should be encouraged. There is often a star quality about her style and personality that will attract attention and admiration.

She is usually headstrong and confident as a child, and will play at being the strong one of any group she is in. She may not know exactly what she wants to be, but she will know she wants to be someone!

The young Filly will be a trifle demanding and may show some temper problems or tantrums. She needs to be taught early in her life that patience is a virtue!

As an adolescent, she is experimental and risk-taking. It is important for her to have open communication with her parents.

HORSE WOMAN AND CAREER

The Horse woman requires a career that is dynamic and stretches her physically and cerebrally. She needs to focus on her way of living because Horses in general have a tendency to get caught up in mundane areas of work and stay there for security.

Any field that allows her to vent her sense of fair play, creativity, and physical energy will make her happy. Good areas include public relations, physical education, veterinarian science, counseling, political activism, media work, photography, charity organization, flight attending or travel consultation, modelling, acting, and education.

The Horse lady should apply herself to her career choice early in life and not pass up any opportunities to further her education, as this will be important for her spiritual satisfaction in later years. Another challenge for the Horse lady is getting paid enough for her efforts. She should always make sure proper pay negotiations take place and that her good work ethic is not taken advantage of.

HORSE WOMAN IN THE TWENTY-FIRST CENTURY

In the twenty-first century, the Horse woman will find her qualities of daring and courage needed to rebuild society. She is a leader, warrior, and pioneer, so whatever field she goes into will benefit from her drive and passionate commitment. She needs to remember that tolerance and patience will increase her powers at this time.

HORSE WOMAN AND SPIRITUALITY

The Horse lady has a great deal of natural respect for the life force energy. Whether she consciously knows this or not, she will have immense empathy for the power and enormity of the life field that surrounds and binds us all together.

Horse women often intuitively take from this energy to replenish their own reserves, and this is a powerful tool for the Horse lady to be aware of. Her own strength is a reflection of her ability to take in the power source around us. This is particularly notable when she finds a cause. She will know no bounds if she learns to utilize this connection of body, spirit, and nature.

She loves nature as a rule, will appreciate its diversity, and will want to be surrounded by it. In her spirituality, the Horse lady finds an anchor to her restless spirit and is able to ground herself. She usually has a distinct belief system that may not necessarily fit a conventional mode, but it will have an impact on those with whom she chooses to share it.

The Horse lady loves myth and grand stories such as those exemplified in the television series *Xena: Warrior Princess*. She relates well to the Warrior Goddess representation in, for example, goddesses like the Gallic Epona and the Celtic fertility goddess Brigantia. As hers is the energy of the young woman, the Horse woman also relates well to the periods of the waxing moon.

RITUAL WORK FOR THE HORSE WOMAN

INVOKING BRIGANTIA FOR LOVE

Ritual Tools
- A wand representing the spear of Brigantia
- A sprig of green ivy
- A bunch of marigolds or sunflowers
- One red and one yellow candle
- One stick of sandalwood incense
- Ritual robes of silver or white
- Likeness or statue of a unicorn

Ritual Time
Waxing moon in Leo.

Relax in a bath or take a long shower, and then dress in your robes. Set up your altar space in your bedroom and place the flowers in a vase on the altar. Entwine the ivy around the base of the candlestick holders or the base of the candles and place the incense in its holder on the altar. Light the incense and candles. Place all of the above items on your altar as offerings to the goddess.

Sitting quietly, invoke the goddess Brigantia by chanting as follows:

"My great goddess Brigantia, I wish to find my love of my life who will be a gentle and committed mate. I ask you to help me reach my highest goals and allow me to gain wisdom and happiness. As you symbolize celebration, I give to you this offering of my peaceful meditation and flowers to invoke your celebratory spirit to assist me in finding the joy I desire."

Sit quietly for a few minutes. Meditate on the light of the candles while visualizing the goddess energy surrounding you and being absorbed through your body to replenish your soul. Then snuff out your candles, promising yourself a relaxing time out in nature as a reward from the goddess.

INVOKING EPONA FOR SPECIAL REQUESTS

Ritual Tools

· A horseshoe or a horseshoe-shaped charm
· One white and one yellow candle
· A craft created by you or a ball of wool
· Sprig from a willow or birch tree
· Handful of pine needles
· One stick each of pine and lemon balm incense
· Ritual robes of silver and white
· An image of a unicorn

Ritual Time

Close to the full moon.

Set up an altar with all of the items listed above with the unicorn image directly in front of you. It can be inside or, if a pleasant night, in a quiet spot of your garden. Light the candles and burn the incense. In your ritual robes, sit quietly on the ground and close your eyes.

Visualize yourself in the moonlight of a peaceful meadow. You look up toward the night sky and see the moonlight shining and dancing through the tall-branched trees surrounding you. You feel soft green grass underneath you.

You are in the middle of this meadow. Now, as you look ahead, a white horse walks gently toward you with the moon shining down above its head. Its eyes are deep and huge and look straight at you with empathy for the beauty and peace you are now feeling. The horse knows you and is returning to be with you to share this peaceful moment.

The horse is now next to you. It bends its head down toward yours as it shares its thoughts with you.

Invoke the goddess Epona by chanting as follows:

> "Oh mother goddess Epona, I request your great protection and help in the following: [*state your request*]. I recognize your power as great mother and warrior spirit. I acknowledge your wisdom and strength.

Help me to curb my headstrong nature so I can be free to reach my proper goals in this lifetime."

Inhale and visualize the power of Epona all around you. Exhale and see yourself pulling free of all restrictions.

Conclude the ritual by saying goodnight till next time to your four-legged friend and snuffing out the candles. Then spread the pine needles out on your altar for the period of the moon. Place the horseshoe, craft or wool, and sprig in a cotton bag to keep as a magickal gift from the goddess and to remind you of her.

MEDITATION FOR CALM AND FOCUSING

Close your eyes and visualize yourself in a beautiful ancient forest. You are sitting underneath an old oak tree. You are also surrounded by other majestic trees under a clear blue sky. There are no clouds for as far as you can see. Nearby is a river and you delight in listening to it. You look up at the sky. The feeling of freedom you have is wonderful.

After a moment, you hear a sound. Turning to your left, you behold a magnificent white horse cantering toward you from quite a distance. Its pace is steady and strong and its carriage dignified. Something deep within you knows it is your special totem and guide. As it gets closer you see it has a horn in the middle of its forehead. You then realize it is no ordinary horse; it is a true white unicorn. You feel amazed and delighted.

The unicorn comes right up to you and kneels, inviting you to mount it. You do so, feeling its strong, supple body. After a moment you grip its mane and the unicorn begins to move slowly around the forest. You feel an amazing connection to this special animal. You are true soul companions and you are united in your love of freedom and purity.

You ride around the forest enjoying the environment. Then you notice your loving friend is taking you somewhere. You see a large house in the distance. The unicorn allows you to dismount as you come to the front of the dwelling.

A wise old woman in warrior garb waits for you at the door. She has a spear in one hand, which she gives you. This is a symbol of your warrior power. You know intuitively that this woman symbolizes part of your warrior self.

She also hands you a scroll with a special message on it. You unfurl it and read the message. It says something deeply personal to you, which only you understand. Take moment to meditate on this message.

The warrior woman leads you around the home, which you realize is your private sanctuary. You love looking in each treasured room. All the rooms contain personal items of yours. You enjoy your time here and remember the way it looks and feels. She tells you to come back any time you need solace or strength, and you know you most definitely will.

When you are ready to leave, the unicorn returns to pick you up and you go back to the old oak tree together. Here you lay the spear down. Your unicorn will keep it for you until you return. You say good-bye.

This place of enchantment and solace can be yours any time you need calm or reflection and can be of true benefit to you.

Tiger Woman
THE NATURAL HUNTRESS

CHARMS AND SYMBOLS

Tarot card:	The Chariot, which represents the victory of the soul
Moon phase:	Waxing
Celestial bodies:	Mars
Herbs and plants:	Dragon's blood, coriander, tiger lily, sunflowers
Colors:	Yellow, gold, orange, ambers
Crystals and gemstones:	Tiger's-eye, amber, leopard skin jasper
Incense:	Dragon's blood, pine, allspice
Lucky day:	Tuesday
Lucky numbers:	9, 18, 27, 36
Ritual colors:	Gold, deep reds
Ritual robes:	Fake furs and animal prints like leopard and tiger
Magickal symbols:	Arrows, cats, panthers, tigers, bears
Goddesses:	The warrior, the huntress, the heroine
Theme song:	"Beauty and the Beast" by Céline Dion and Peabo Bryson

ASSOCIATED GODDESSES fOR THE TIGER WOMAN

Sekhmet: This lioness-headed goddess of ancient Egypt embodies the ferocity, daring, and courage of the true Tiger woman. She is also called the "Powerful One." Sekhmet, Hathor, and Isis form the Egyptian Triple Goddess. Sekhmet was warlike, but also held the qualities of a healer and was linked to human destiny.

Ishtar: Mesopotamian goddess whose associated animal is the lion. She displayed great anger and love. She is said to have forced her way into the underworld to rescue her lover, and could be extremely fierce and threatening.

Kali: Hindu mythology associates the tiger with this great goddess of destruction and rebirth, attraction and sexuality.

Durga: This Indian goddess is often depicted riding a tiger, symbolizing regal power. Her other symbols are the buffalo and the lion.

POSITIVE TRAITS

initiating	devoted
feisty	daring
caring	ambitious
quick-acting	ethical
trusting	energetic
dedicated	direct
brave	creative
enthusiastic	discriminating
passionate	bold
idealistic	romantic
optimistic	determined

NEGATIVE TRAITS

domineering	headstrong
interfering	impulsive
rigid	argumentative
naive	foolhardy
excessive	intolerant
impetuous	compulsive
judgmental	bullying
overactive	scattered
unjust	reckless
unrealistic	obsessional
self-deceiving	dictatorial

fAMOUS TIGER WOMEN

Mary Queen of Scots · Diana Rigg · Queen Elizabeth II · Demi Moore
Agatha Christie · Marilyn Monroe · Cybill Shepherd · Jodie Foster
Rosie O'Donnell · Elisabeth Kübler-Ross · Germaine Greer · Norma Shearer
Penélope Cruz · Hilary Swank · Crystal Gayle · Emily Brontë

TIGER WOMAN'S NUMBER

1 A leading lady Tiger, you are naturally born to rule and oversee others. You may need to make time in your life for family and intimate partnerships. Watch the desire to dominate!

2 You are very interested in a mate and will be quite the gentle pussycat at times. Your intuition is powerful and you love to act as peacemaker. Occasionally you will need to watch that others are not draining your energy source from you.

3 A Tiger with a mouth! You love to talk to others and will be a great communicator. You could also do well in investigative journalism or any area that requires guts and drive.

4 A hardworking feline! You like structure in your life, though your Tiger qualities of impulsiveness and overambition sometimes make your lifestyle hectic. Watch rigid attitudes.

5 You are a free-spirited Tiger. You enjoy the limelight and may have dramatic flair! You have artistic abilities and should keep your options open. Travel features strongly.

6 A harmonious home life is very important to you. You will be very interested in children and your mate and will pay attention to detail. You may fret a bit, however, as a Tiger with a conscience.

7 You will have strong needs to stand out and succeed in your own endeavors. Career will be important and you will value your private time.

8 Tiger ladies with strong ambitions are born with the number 8. You are the natural executive or head of an enterprise. Your private life could suffer, so be careful.

9 A dynamic cat! You love to lead and your Tiger energy will be very powerful. Politics will attract you and you will be very particular in your choice of mate.

THE HUNTRESS!

The poet William Blake symbolized the Tiger's fire energy in his poem "The Tyger": "Tyger, tyger, burning bright in the forests of the night." Feisty, fearless, and feline, the Tiger woman courageously carries an often-heavy load through the forests of her life.

The Tiger woman is the natural hunter and protector bestowed with all the gifts of the goddess Sekhmet, the Egyptian goddess of battle and war. The Tiger woman embodies the charisma, strength, and boldness of the goddess spirit and displays these traits in an often old-fashioned, glamour-and-sparkle kind of way! Her energy is formidable and awesome.

Tiger woman Agatha Christie created two of the greatest fictional sleuths of all time: Detective Hercule Pierot and the unfathomable Miss Marples. Tiger woman Diana Rigg portrayed the sleek, feline Avenger to perfection in her famous television series, while Marilyn Monroe captured her audience with charming yet powerful charisma.

Tiger woman Queen Elizabeth II has maintained her role as England's monarch for over half a century. Her continuing shows of strength and fortitude in troubled times demonstrate the protective, enduring spirit the Tiger character stands for. Germaine Greer, a Tiger woman, has fought courageously for women's rights for several decades. And Tiger woman Elisabeth Kübler-Ross revolutionized our understanding of death and dying in her pioneering work as a psychiatrist with terminally ill patients and in her spiritual focus as a scientist.

In the Tiger woman there is a primordial desire to hunt for what she perceives as her brood. She may give the appearance of stalking her prey because of the restless, strong-willed, and focused way with which she attempts to secure her targets and goals.

She does, however, have a gentler side to her personality that is deeply emotional and sentimental. She has an overriding sense of protection for those she considers part of her pack. The Tiger woman believes her role is primarily to guard, and she places herself in risky positions to defend and hunt down the enemy.

Because her energy and willpower is so unnervingly strong, it can border on the obsessive and impetuous. The Tiger woman can have a stronger-than-usual masculine energy, which may encourage others to react to her in a negative or threatening way. She may find herself stalked or preyed upon by others who feel threatened by her expression of herself.

Although the Tiger woman is generally strong-willed, she may still fall victim to tricksters or shysters who prey on her vulnerable side. Some Tigers never quite grow up completely from their cub stage, entertaining a sense of false security when dealing with others. This emotional naivety can cost the Tiger dearly if she doesn't learn to protect her skin.

Her unrealistic sense of self-power and energetic reserve may cause the Tiger woman to think she is above human frailty. She needs to slow down, reflect, and invite patience and moderation into her day-to-day life. Otherwise, she may end up chasing her own tail and burning herself out!

The warrior side of Tiger's energy is well developed. This may be a double-edged sword. Although this quality gives her extreme drive in whatever she chooses to do, it can also leave her open to total exhaustion and breakdown if she does not take care of herself. However, the Tiger woman's passion and sense of justice are extremely potent tools for good. With all of her strength, she is basically a romantic and creative creature who requires regular pats on the head and applause in order to feel her happiest.

Rushing in where angels fear to tread is a common problem for the Tiger woman who can also be too headstrong, overdominating, impulsive, and foolhardy. Two Tiger women who illustrate this point are Marilyn Monroe and Mary Queen of Scots. Marilyn Monroe flirted with forces beyond her control in her associations with men and her involvement with drugs. She did not heed the dangers she faced and her fate was to be tragically overpowered. Mary Queen of Scots epitomizes the Tiger's fighting spirit as well as her naivety in her unsuccessful attempts to take over the English throne. All Tiger women need to acknowledge their daredevil traits and learn to understand themselves more deeply before they, too, end up in a situation where they can't see the forest for the trees.

What sometimes seems a forced period of introspection and self-development can result in the Tiger woman's hastened spiritual evolvement. This gives her the flexibility and empowerment to reach the full potential she is really meant to hunt. As she is a noble protector and defender of the weak, she can find fulfillment in a variety of careers and lifestyle situations where her innate courage is appreciated.

The Tiger woman's love for challenges and danger can be harnessed into a powerful force for good if she so chooses. She may, however, sometimes be dismayed when she finds herself the loser in competitive situations with her sister signs. Although she does not lose the battle from lack of courage, she does often miss the subtler blows of competition that only feminine tricks and maneuvers can produce. She needs to sharpen her powers of feminine wiles to match those of her competitors.

The Tiger woman also should be careful of her capacity to frighten others with the emotional ferocity she inherits from her Warrior Goddess power. She should think of the terrible warlike aspect of the goddess Sekhmet or Kali to realize she can do a lot of damage. Interestingly, the Tiger woman is often oblivious to this warlike aspect of hers and can be genuinely puzzled as to why others are afraid or in awe of her. She must realize she can display this ferocious trait and learn that her anger can alienate her from others quickly. This will leave her alone in life if she does not learn to bring in her sharp claws and lower her fearful growl.

The Tiger woman enchants and enthralls us all with her courage, but she can evoke real fear if she wants to show she is not a pussycat! At other times though, this wilder side needs to be tamed and she should cultivate her gentler and more reflective tendencies to quell her fiery energy. Meditation, various forms of prayer, or chanting to music can prove relaxing for Tigers who benefit from the soothing of their fierce passions.

To release the Tiger woman's true nobility and potential requires a deep spiritual value system coupled with development of her inner faith and detachment from her intense passions. Ignoring these values will only cause her to suffer. Deep introspection will help her get in touch with her animal side, which needs some solid taming to fully benefit her. It is good advice for the Tiger woman to learn about her warrior traits early in life to appreciate how she can help others.

TIGER WOMAN AND LOVE

Paradoxically, the Tiger woman can easily become the hunted in this delicate area of her life. Her passions and vulnerable traits can become her worst enemies, leaving her open to cruel or weak partners who desire only her rich Tiger skin to decorate their floor. In Tiger woman Emily Brontë's literary masterpiece *Wuthering*

Heights, Master Heathcliff captured the heroine Cathy and emotionally skinned her alive with his cruel character.

The obsessive and compulsive way the Tiger goes after what she wants can mean she is prey to her own emotional demands. She often falls for weaker, non-committed mates who need her strength and heroism. Alternatively, she may also have a tendency to partner with dangerous mates with addictive personalities who appeal to her sexuality.

The Tiger woman is seeking a strong partner of inner conviction and passion who can also offer her a safe sanctuary and protection. Only a very secure mate can cope with her extreme views and moods. At the same time, her partner needs to be gentle enough to soothe her savage beast within. This is not an ordinary partner!

The Tiger woman usually suffers a number of early wounds in her search for a mate, and can spend a number of years single before she meets her equal. Jodie Foster, for example, has lived a full life as a very independent Tiger!

It is often a terrible shock to the idealistic and straightforward Tiger woman to discover her mate is not the person she perceived him or her to be. Agatha Christie's first husband allegedly turned out to be a weak philanderer who betrayed and hurt her deeply. Agatha reportedly went through a very dark night of the soul when she discovered the truth about her husband and disappeared from public view for quite some time. However, her second husband was a passionate archeologist who shared her interests and suited her strong spirit. He became her true friend and lover, and their union lasted many happy years.

The myth of Beauty and the Beast has poignant relevance for the Tiger woman. The power of the Warrior Goddess proves a valuable teacher in recognizing dark energy in ourselves that may inadvertently attract the wrong type of people. It also helps us recognize the negativity in others. As the Tiger woman matures to develop patience, balance, and a sense of strength, she proves to be an endearing and irreplaceable mate.

As a wife and mother, the Tiger woman will go out of her way to protect and care for all. She can be strict with her offspring, expecting them to obey and respect her authority. She needs to develop sensitivity to their feelings. Yet she is extremely proud of her loved ones and will be the first family member to acknowledge and show off their accomplishments.

Tiger Woman and Compatibility

Tiger & Rat
♡♡

Can work, but Rat may have secret agendas and Tiger demands honesty.

Tiger & Ox
♡♡

Good for endurance, but Tiger may need a bit more excitement. Ox feels Tiger is too feisty at times.

Tiger & Tiger
♡♡

Difficult, but passionate! These two definitely understand each other, but both like to be chief!

Tiger & Cat
♡

Difficult union; a lot of sulks likely. Cat feels drawn to Tiger's passion, however.

Tiger & Dragon
♡♡♡

Good, as both respect each other's strength. They usually love acting out king and queen.

Tiger & Snake
♡

Difficult union as the Snake is on the deceptive side and Tiger is aware of it.

Tiger & Horse
♡♡♡

Quite positive. Tiger loves the challenge of settling Horse down.

Tiger & Goat
♡

These two attract each other, but Goat is too procrastinating for Tiger.

Tiger & Monkey
♡

Good if Monkey lays off the games. Tiger likes to feel she has the upper hand, but Monkey dominates.

Tiger & Rooster
♡

Fun, however the two energies seem to lack stability. Rooster needs a lot of attention, which Tiger resents.

Tiger & Dog
♡♡♡

Devoted Dog is Tiger's best friend. Dog has the interests of his or her mate at heart.

Tiger & Pig
♡♡

Tiger admires Pig's drive. However, Tiger may become upset with Pig's forcefulness.

♡♡♡♡ = excellent   ♡♡♡ = good   ♡♡ = fair   ♡ = difficult

Sometimes she can be a little too rigid as a parent. It is important to loosen up a bit and keep her sense of humor and play. Her ability to play with her offspring is a lovable characteristic!

Even if the Tiger woman does not have children of her own she will take a strong interest in young ones and spend much of her energy in activities involving children.

TIGER WOMAN AND HEALTH

The Tiger woman often burns the candle at both ends. She is vital and has very good endurance for long working hours, but suffers from exhaustion and nervous tension if overworked.

Her nature is to stalk and prey, so she finds it difficult to relax. Music therapy can be very beneficial for her as she loves dancing. Many Tiger women also love animals and enjoy having more than one dog or domestic animal as playmates to relax and exercise with. She would do well to find a sport or recreational hobby that is unrelated to her career to engage in so she can learn to dissociate from her work routine and genuinely relax for a while.

Areas of health for the Tiger woman to watch are circulation, skin sensitivity, and muscular stiffness. Viral infections should be speedily treated to avoid chest complaints.

TIGER WOMAN AND FINANCES

The Tiger woman's earning capacity is usually powerful as she is geared toward success in the outer world and prepared to fight for opportunities. She is not averse to competition in her work area and has good staying power.

Normally a good saver, the Tiger woman likes to provide security for her close ones. She may, however, be a bit fixed in her ideas about finances and can afford to be more flexible. Her main luck can come from real estate.

TIGER WOMAN AS A CHILD

The Tiger woman is very active and strong-minded as a child. As a young cub she will enjoy all aspects of play and recreation, but with a tendency toward creative activities, including artwork and any subject working with the hands.

She loves competitive sports and participates well in a team environment. The Tiger child needs gentle handling, however, as she has a very sensitive side that hungers for appreciation and paternal support. She respects firmness in a parent, but will rebel if treated in an authoritarian way. The little Tigress is not a particularly patient child, and may show signs of willfulness or temper, which may require a strong dose of disciplinary action to tame.

She is usually a very popular child surrounded by many playmates. She may, however, go through a fairly painful adolescence with the occasional emotional drama as she grapples with the emerging warrior energy.

TIGER WOMAN AND CAREER

The Tiger woman is happy involved in a male-dominated career, as she is naturally attracted to authority. She connects well, therefore, to pioneering or managerial roles and has an attraction to the police force or the armed services. She also does well in leading academic work.

Likely career choices are government manager, policewoman, army or air force personnel, detective, special investigator, company manager, medical practitioner, psychologist, dentist, physiotherapist, expert analyzer, lawyer or administrator, and physical educator. The Tiger woman is not suited to menial or subservient roles, and needs mentally and physically active work to keep her involved.

TIGER WOMAN IN THE TWENTY-FIRST CENTURY

The Tiger will be discovering new frontiers of every kind in the twenty-first century—spiritual and physical—and may well be at the forefront of political and social change. As she is both a rebel and an authoritarian in her energy, she will be very attracted to changing society and introducing new concepts of womanhood and spirituality. In a real sense, her dynamic warrior spirit is part of the new age. Her interest in the young and the vulnerable will propel many Tigers into careers in the public eye.

TIGER WOMAN AND SPIRITUALITY

The Tiger woman is often too absorbed with the external world to direct her mind to the more subtle aspects of spirituality and female psychology that would help her deal with her unique personality. However, it is within this area that she can gain the most strength in life if she wishes to.

Because the Tiger woman epitomizes the huntress, she relates well to the goddess energies of hunting and fertility. With her capacity to be powerful and her innate creative or destructive qualities, she also relates to the goddess power of Sekhmet, the lioness-headed goddess of destruction and liberation.

RITUAL WORK FOR THE TIGER WOMAN

INVOKING SEKHMET FOR PROSPERITY AND LUCK

Ritual Tools

· A piece of emulated or fake animal skin material
· One tiger's-eye stone
· One piece of amber
· A statue, drawing, or likeness of Sekhmet, the lioness-headed goddess
· One stick each of lemon balm and myrrh incense
· One gold and one yellow candle
· Tiger's-eye pendant or other piece of jewelry

Ritual Time

Waxing moon.

Create an altar in a private place with the tools listed above. Meditate on the awesome animal power and charisma of the tiger or lion while lighting the incense and candles. Draw your energy and spirit power from within you and chant the following to invoke the goddess:

> "Oh powerful goddess Sekhmet, protector and healer of your people, I take from your strength and echo its warmth within my own being. Help me to curb my destructive qualities and develop my innate power as a healer. Assist me to reach my goals [*state intentions here*] if they accord directly with my soul's progress. I acknowledge the power of the lion spirit within myself. I honor this power which stands directly in the goddess path."

Conclude your ritual by snuffing out the candles and incense. Wear the jewelry or have the gemstones close to you whenever you wish to meditate on your inner power.

INVOKING KALI FOR LOVE

Ritual Tools
· A wand made of yellow agate or yellow material
· A vase of sunflowers
· A tiger's-eye stone
· Three yellow candles
· Rose and ylang-ylang oil
· Ritual garment of animal print material

Ritual Time
Waxing moon in Libra.

Make an altar with the above tools. Burn a few drops of the oils in an oil burner while you take a bath or shower. Dress in the ritual garments and light the candles.

Take the wand in hand and invoke the goddess Kali by chanting the following:

"Oh great goddess, I honor your sacred connection to men and women. I request your help in bringing to me a mate who will respect my strength and honor my goodwill. I ask that I be not blinded by emotions but that my spirit will connect to the right soul mate. I acknowledge your ability as a huntress to find the right partner for me."

Conclude the ritual by snuffing out the candles. Leave the items on your altar for one lunar month in honor of the goddess.

MEDITATION FOR CALM AND FOCUSING

Close your eyes and visualize standing in a valley surrounded by huge mountains. The mountains are covered in tall trees, and all around you is the sound of birdsong. You look at every mountain and you see a pathway leading from the base to the summit.

Now choose a mountain and begin to walk up its pathway. At this point think of an issue that is causing you pain or confusion, see that issue at the top of the summit, and as you approach the top, believe that you can face that issue and deal with it calmly and confidently. You will not be afraid, you will not worry if you cannot solve it today, but you will be able to face it.

Now you are at the top. You look, but the problem has disappeared. You look at the sky; it is beautifully clear and you feel so alive and energized that you could almost fly off the top and touch all the surrounding summits. Now you glance down to the valley floor below, and there you see your issue—it has fallen to the ground. It looks so very small now from where you are standing.

With this new perspective, you can confidently walk back down to the valley and realize that a problem is only as bad as where you place it in your life. You decide whether it is insurmountable or something that life presents to teach us to rise above. Stay a while on the summit until you feel rested, then go face that challenge head-on. Don't worry if you can't solve it this time, just have confidence in knowing you have climbed many mountains before and you will climb many more.

Everyone has their own special mountain that they can retreat to; go there whenever you feel a need to regenerate. Lost your way? It's easy; the path is in your head!

PART V

Dark Goddess Women

Rat Woman

THE NATURAL BEWITCHER

CHARMS AND SYMBOLS

Tarot card:	The Magician, which represents skill and wisdom
Moon phase:	Waxing to full moon
Celestial bodies:	Pluto, the moon
Herbs and plants:	Wheat, nightshade, hemlock
Colors:	Reds, blacks, purples
Crystals and gemstones:	Obsidian, ruby, clear quartz
Incense:	Jasmine, sandalwood
Lucky day:	Thursday
Lucky numbers:	7, 13
Ritual colors:	Ruby, purple
Ritual robes:	Velvets, silks, satins, fabrics with sparkle
Magickal symbols:	Pentacles, owls, crystal balls
Goddesses:	The mystics, the clairvoyant, the bewitcher
Theme song:	"Rhiannon" by Fleetwood Mac

ASSOCIATED GODDESSES FOR THE RAT WOMAN

Persephone: Greek goddess who descended to the underworld and became the bride of Lord Hades. She is associated with rebirth, the magick of the hidden and dark, new life, and regeneration. Persephone was said to spend one third of the year (winter) in the lower world and the fertile time in the upper to balance the seasons.

Ianna: Sumerian goddess who also descended to the underworld to save her city and people. She is associated with power, bravery, and the ability to survive death.

Lilith: Biblical goddess of the night and magick. Her name is said to be a derivative of the Sumerian goddess Belit-ili. She is associated with female sexuality, and was said to be the Divine Lady to the Canaanites.

POSITIVE TRAITS

warm	psychic
charismatic	intuitive
passionate	literate
dynamic	family-orientated
stylish	astute
determined	reliable
pioneering	disciplined
adaptable	enduring

NEGATIVE TRAITS

controlling	overbearing
compulsive	hyperactive
materialistic	hoarding
egocentric	overambitious
obsessive	anxious
oversensitive	clannish
deceitful	pedantic
thin-skinned	nervous

FAMOUS RAT WOMEN

(the late) Queen Mother · Charlotte Brontë · Lauren Bacall
Margaret Mitchell · Olivia Newton-John · Mata Hari · Daryl Hannah
Lucrezia Borgia · Stevie Nicks · Sinéad Cusack · Margot Kidder
Alyssa Milano · Gwyneth Paltrow · Toni Collette · Kristen Scott Thomas
Cameron Diaz · Jennie Garth · Nancy Wake · Tracy Pollan

RAT WOMAN'S NUMBER

1 A leading Rat lady! You are capable of lending a great deal of pioneering drive in any enterprise. Great combination for the entrepreneur!

2 Sentimental Rat lady! You love home and family and are particularly sensitive to others—their emotional happiness is of concern to you.

3 You have the definite gift of gab and are able to talk your way out of any trap!

4 A Rat that builds foundations, security is your number one priority and you will work hard to achieve this. You have special needs for stability.

5 This is a versatile combo. You will be very vivacious and energetic and will have strong needs to explore!

6 Home-loving yet ambitious, you make a powerful partner or ally. You are super sensitive and can be a bit too thin-skinned, so watch those emotions and extremes!

7 Clairvoyant Ms. Rat! You have finely tuned whiskers and seem to pick up vibes from everywhere! Learn to develop your psychic side and avoid extremes. As a perfectionist Rat you need to sail your own boat and should seek self-employment.

8 The Rat with drive! You function well in situations of authority and may be a bit of a tycoon Rat!

9 You are very intellectual and will succeed in any endeavor that involves mental activity and quick clarity of thought.

THE BEWITCHER!

Why is the Rat woman a natural witch? How long have you got? A woman born in the year of the Rat has many of the qualities of the Dark Goddess, such as profound insight, remarkable intuition, clairvoyant powers, and pure magickal energy!

Take a look at some of the Rat women of history: the sheer courage of the late Queen Mother, who shone perhaps her brightest during the dark days of World War II; the brilliance of writers like Margaret Mitchell and Charlotte Brontë; the exotic fascination of renowned spy Mata Hari; the bravery and inspirational courage of Olivia Newton-John; the allure of Lauren Bacall and Alyssa Milano (star of *Charmed*); or the bravery of Nancy Wake (also known as the "White Mouse"), the decorated war heroine. The Rat woman is a creature of extraordinary passion, intellect, and imagination.

To call the Rat woman a survivor is an understatement. Her amazing capacity to brave the elements, take on risks, and make the grade is formidable and sometimes even alarming. To quote the legendary character Scarlett O'Hara from the movie version of Margaret Mitchell's novel *Gone with the Wind:* "If I have to lie, steal, cheat, or kill . . . I'll never be hungry again!" This typifies this sign's courageous spirit and energy.

In Chinese astrology, the rat is linked intrinsically to the hidden and the night. The Rat woman's power is very much just as secretive and surprising. Often a superb shape-shifter, the Rat woman's energy can be somewhat deceptive to others.

For instance, Mata Hari showed one aspect of her personality with her exotic dancing, and another in her spy work as a double agent. Another famous and highly acclaimed Rat spy is the White Mouse. A journalist and writer, Nancy Wake was also a superb shape-shifter and defied the traps of the Nazis over and over again.

Rat woman Charlotte Brontë also had a hidden personality. She was, on the one hand, a demure vicar's daughter who displayed all the virtuous characteristics thought suitable for her time. On the other hand, however, she was a writer of incredible passion, insight, and depth. Jane Eyre, Charlotte's heroine in the novel of the same name, was an apparently plain governess, but underneath she held all the insight of a true clairvoyant! Similarly, Scarlett O'Hara, the creation of Margaret Mitchell in *Gone with the Wind,* was much more than a delicate Southern belle. These Rat authors mirrored qualities intrinsic to all Rat women in their brilliant fictional characters.

There is a negative side to the Rat woman, however, that she should learn to control. Her very strengths can become her greatest weaknesses until she begins to know herself. Mata Hari, for example, fell into the trap of passionately loving a man who ultimately betrayed her. She became so seduced by her own power that she lost her life; she played the role of a double agent to her detriment.

The Rat woman's inner weaknesses of compulsiveness, anxiety, self-deception, and trickery could lead her into times of peril. She must learn to face these demons and overcome them with the inner strength she possesses. Otherwise, she may lose her way, forget her intuition, allow herself to drown in her emotions, and lose all perspective. Her discernment and intellect will degenerate into criticism and perfectionism, and her creativity will waste away.

As with all signs, self-knowledge and self-empowerment are the greatest powers one can pursue and have. With temperance and wisdom, the Rat woman has all the potential to make a powerful contribution to the world around her and prove an inspirational force to others. Like Scarlett O'Hara, she is the natural heroine. She refuses to give up and believes implicitly in fighting for what she believes in.

In my life experience, I have met some outstanding examples of Rat women whose courage and ingenuity are an inspiration to all. However, life or fate often hands them some powerful challenges, which they must learn to overcome. Through this experience, Rat women learn to face adversity with courage. With their natural attributes, Rat women can and do survive to develop inherent wisdom.

The Rat woman is protective of her loved ones, but needs to be careful of becoming overly interested in their welfare. It is vitally important for her to have a creative or mental outlet to vent her strong-willed energy in a constructive way.

In her younger years, the Rat woman may find herself involved with people who will teach her about some of the negative sides of human nature. These relations may subsequently leave her drained and disillusioned. Like the goddess Persephone, she seems destined to experience the underworld as part of her spiritual journey. If the Rat woman is wise, she will not allow these early experiences to embitter her outlook on life. She will take whatever she has learnt from the experiences to better cope with any adversity life presents.

Although the Rat woman is enchanting, bewitching, and magickal, she is just a human after all. The most important challenge for the Rat woman is learning about her duality. She has the divine spirit within her, and a study into the powerful effects of the Dark Goddess will benefit her enormously in mastering her lessons for spiritual evolution. She is the pioneer who, like the goddess Persephone, can turn the world around if she so desires!

RAT WOMAN AND LOVE

What is love for the Rat woman? Is it a compulsion, an obsession, a chance to lose herself in her seductive powers? Or is it a case of true mind-and-body connection? Learning emotional discernment is such an important life lesson for the Rat woman it should be taught to her as a child. Like Scarlett O'Hara, the Rat woman must avoid allowing her romantic spirit to rule her.

The Rat woman often yearns for the unattainable ideal and may waste her life searching for this elusive character. She will use extraordinary amounts of energy, time, and anything else she can offer to win his or her affections. Unfortunately, with this immense surge of energy and unbridled determination, the Rat woman can often lose sight of what she really needs. She can only truly respect a strong-willed partner who has learned to accept and control his or her dark side in a responsible way. Other mates that she may find herself attracted to will often lack this level of maturity and will ultimately become incompatible with this strong woman.

In real life, the Rat woman often finds herself involved with partners that have a certain air of sophistication and inner control about them. Over time, however, she may begin to discern real worth in people she becomes attached to.

The Rat woman has all the lethal charm at her disposal to make anyone fall in love with her. This includes her finely tuned psychic sense and intuition. Unfortunately, if she is not careful, this very deep capacity to delve into the psyches of those around her can tempt her to seduce and control others. This will not bring her the happiness she seeks.

Intellectual sharing, compatibility of interests, and mutual respect are the real ingredients for a successful union for the Rat woman. If she listens to the voice of her

Rat Woman and Compatibility

Rat & Rat
♡♡♡

Flirty, fun, and warm. Watch honesty between these two! They tend to become very successful together.

Rat & Ox
♡♡♡

Dependable Ox and exciting Rat can be a successful team if Rat stays attached. Ox will need to open up more emotionally though.

Rat & Tiger
♡♡

Tiger is a wee bit too dominating for Rat, who wants to be boss! Difficult ties are likely.

Rat & Cat
♡

Rat and Cat face grave difficulties in avoiding marital or partnership woes, as Rat won't always heed Cat's constant desire to be pampered. This is not a good bet!

Rat & Dragon
♡♡♡

Dragon can be strong, which Rat respects. With mutual admiration—a likely ingredient in this union—it can last.

Rat & Snake
♡♡

Seductive Snake has sex appeal, but way too many other partners! Rat will suffer anxiety. A sexy dalliance however!

Rat & Horse
♡

Forget this one. Horse is too self-centered, and Rat will lose here. Money issues can create problems.

Rat & Goat
♡

Difficult combination as Rat loves excitement while Goat longs for peace and quiet. Rat will not appreciate the Goat's lack of decisiveness.

Rat & Monkey
♡

Monkey is charming, but Rat will not appreciate the deceptions Monkey loves to play. A volatile union is likely here.

Rat & Rooster
♡♡

Can work as Rooster has energy and charm, as long as they can compromise as a pair.

Rat & Dog
♡♡♡

Can be very endearing. They are true soul mates, but Rat likes to lead. Dog has a protective side that attracts Rat.

Rat & Pig
♡♡♡

Pig has a domineering side that annoys Rat, but Rat loves the loyalty of Pig.

♡♡♡♡ = excellent   ♡♡♡ = good   ♡♡ = fair   ♡ = difficult

innate intuition, she will avoid the pitfalls of those who seek to charm and seduce her. She would be well advised to heed this early on in her many relationships.

As a wife and mother, the Rat woman can be superlative as she devotes herself to the care and nurturing of her family. As a mother, she is incredibly interested in her young, yet again she must be aware of the "dark mother" syndrome. Some Rat woman mothers can estrange themselves from their own children with overanxiety and an inability to cut the maternal threads at the appropriate time. This is a particularly sad outcome for the emotional Rat who adores her brood over anything else in life.

Self-sacrifice is a double-edged sword for the Rat woman who must practice balance in her desire to hold and maintain the security of love that she so desires from her family. She must also be careful of criticizing her loved ones, even when she does so from a well-meaning, protective way. Learning to allow her children freedom of expression and choice will keep her close to them.

RAT WOMAN AND HEALTH

The Rat woman's stamina can be very enduring and vital. In the rat race of everyday life, she usually comes out in front. However, she needs to take care that she does not overdo things and leave herself open to exhaustion and nervous tension.

On the other hand, the Rat woman has a great capacity to repair her ills and usually bounces back after a short rest period. Acupuncture, herbal medicine, and natural remedies work well for her, and she can benefit from Reiki therapy, meditation, and yoga.

The Rat woman can be anxious about health issues in times of emotional stress. This can lead to worrying herself into an illness, so she needs to relax and adopt a healthy regime to avoid tension. Lots of fresh vegetables and herbs in her diet assist nervous disorders associated with irritable bowel and stomach complaints.

RAT WOMAN AND FINANCES

The Rat woman loves to hoard and is a confirmed shopper. She loves to buy or accumulate products and may be subject to having too much clutter! She loves to hoard expensive items and may spend her savings too quickly. She needs to develop a sensible investment plan.

The Rat woman tends to do better on her own rather than in business with others. Care must be taken that others don't try to take advantage of her good fortune, and she must watch business partnerships carefully.

RAT WOMAN AS A CHILD

This child will have a combination of enchantment and magick as well as an old soul quality, which will amaze all those who meet her. Creative, perceptive, charming, and eager, she will show off her personality eagerly.

The Rat child is strong-willed and a natural witch, so watch out: she will wind you around her fingers! She will have a built-in desire to be successful and is a born achiever.

This child is subject to many changes of mood and can have a strong temper. She needs to learn discipline. The power of her emotions can take over and she needs appropriate outlets to vent her energy constructively. Otherwise, she may have the odd temper tantrum to free up all that psychic power!

The Rat child should be involved with creative activities to encourage her intuition. She will naturally be extremely curious about life and people and will often display astonishing insight beyond her years. If she does not take to a new person, take notice as the Rat child usually has a good reason why!

RAT WOMAN AND CAREER

What *can't* a Rat woman do? One Rat woman I know is never still. Her incredible vitality finds its outlets in a number of activities, including running her own business, charity work, and training young people in the musical field. The Rat woman's energy fits well into these liberated times.

The Rat woman's keen sense of insight and her ability to pick up on interesting facts and aspects around her make her an ideal woman in any job that requires intuition and exceptional powers of observation. For this reason, her career should be mentally rather than physically oriented. The Rat loves mental stimulation and analytical discussion. She needs a position that will provide potential for mind expansion and growth.

The Rat woman also tends to love learning the psychology of others and of herself. For this reason she is well suited to jobs that combine plenty of opportunity to study her own interests as well as helping others.

Good career choices for Rat ladies include media, journalism, public relations, computer information training, public administration, clairvoyance, tarot reading, psychology, astrology, writing, teaching, counseling, Reiki therapy, massage therapy, acting, or running a small business of her own .

RAT WOMAN IN THE TWENTY-FIRST CENTURY

The twenty-first century will be a time of challenge for the Rat woman, who knows instinctively the power of the goddess within. If she follows her instincts, strong opportunities for self-advancement can result. She has a need to be a pioneer and leader. She will instigate new ways of thinking in the twenty-first century and will be found in the arts, government, the media, and all areas of spiritual development.

RAT WOMAN AND SPIRITUALITY

The Rat woman discovers her attunement to the metaphysical world at a very young age and relates naturally to the profound study of spirituality in later life. She often finds spirituality a fascinating field of interest, and can easily find life fulfillment in the area of spiritual guidance and counseling.

Most Rat women I have met convey their individual experiences of the spirit world and have been deeply moved by its effects on their personal belief systems and lives. One Rat woman told me of her experience with an astrological reader. The reader said the Rat woman would meet someone of a different race and culture in a foreign country who would be her true soul mate. She did indeed travel to another country to work shortly after, and within a few months she met her husband-to-be. She knew instantly that they would spend a very long and happy life together. His background was exactly what the reader had foretold.

Rat woman Nancy Wake had a special fate foretold for her by a Maori woman. The woman predicted that Nancy would lead an extraordinary life as recounted in her recent biography. The wise woman saw a destiny of greatness for the young child, who would one day win international medals for her war bravery. Similarly, the late Queen Mother, dubbed "the most dangerous woman in Europe" by Hitler, also had her fortune told with chilling accuracy. A psychic told her when she was six years old that she would one day wear a crown on her head.

The power of the Dark Goddess sign gives the Rat woman amazing access to her hidden spiritual realm. She can therefore benefit from detailed studies of psychic and intuitive development techniques. Learning how to read the tarot and astrological aspects or studying spiritual psychology will assist the Rat woman and guide her on her spiritual pathway.

In addition, as the Rat woman can relate to the symbolic journeys of empowerment undertaken by goddesses like Persephone and Ianna, she is well advised to learn more about their respective myths. This will assist her in exploring the divine feminine in herself.

RITUAL WORK FOR THE RAT WOMAN

INVOKING IANNA FOR PROSPERITY AND GOOD FORTUNE

Ritual Tools

· A black feather
· One black and one white candle
· One piece each of obsidian and clear quartz
· One stick each of jasmine and sandalwood incense
· Ritual robes of velvet, silk, or satin

Ritual Time

In the evening, preferably with the moon waning.

In the quiet of a private room, dress in your robes and meditate on whatever issues are pressing in your life at this time: a relationship, a career decision, or whatever. Then arrange the black feather, the crystals, the incense, and the candles on your altar. Light the candles and incense and chant the following to invoke the goddess Ianna:

> "Goddess Ianna, I invoke your help in achieving my purpose [*state your intentions here*]. As a Rat woman, I honor your qualities of intuition and resourcefulness. I accept my capacity to transpose both the outer and inner worlds of my realm. I renounce all my fears and detach from my emotional conflicts. I accept your divine power and assistance. Guide me on the winding path of life so that I may express my greatest gifts to honor the power of the Goddess. Help me to resolve my issues in the way that is right for my soul's growth."

Conclude your ritual by giving thanks to the goddess, burning the incense, and snuffing out the candles. Allow an answer to come to you gently in time.

INVOKING LILITH FOR LOVE AND SEDUCTION

Ritual Tools

· A small, pink, rose quartz wand
· A silver chalice or cup full of water
· A glass filled with red wine
· One pink and one red candle
· Jasmine and geranium incense
· Ritual robes of velvet, satin, or silk

Ritual Time

Waxing to full moon.

After bathing, dress in your ritual robes and relax. Arrange the tools listed on your altar and light the candles and incense. Invoke the goddess by chanting the following:

> "Great goddess Lilith, I invoke your power and protection. I am searching for a mate who will be strong yet respectful of my being to accompany me through the journeys of my life. Help me to send my thoughts out to the right person and let that person enter my life freely and passionately."

Honor the goddess by drinking a toast to her life force with the red wine. Conclude the ritual by snuffing out the candles and incense and releasing the petition to the guidance of fulfillment.

MEDITATION FOR COMPANIONSHIP AND RELAXATION

Relax and close your eyes. Visualize a large, long pathway. At the end of this pathway is a gate. You enter through the gateway and see a table set with food and wine and two empty chairs.

Walk now to the table. It is full of all the foods you like to eat. There is a full vase of fresh flowers on the table and music that you like playing softly in the background. Sit down, and in your meditative dream close your eyes. In your mind see the person you want to know sitting on the seat opposite you. This person is what you make him or her to be. Instill this person with the qualities you are searching for in a companion and friend. Then open your eyes and see that person smiling back at you seated on the chair.

Talk now to this person and feel happy and relaxed for he or she is responding to you with like kindness and warmth. At the end of the meal, walk out of the gate together, say good-bye, and know your paths will cross again.

Alternative: If you would like to meditate on an issue or de-stress yourself, simply have one chair at your table and sit and eat and drink in relaxation. Invite whomever you would like to share your meal, and see those that cause you pain far, far away in another place. You know only that they exist somewhere else and they cannot touch you here. When you have had enough time for now, finish your meal and walk back out through that gate to where you face the challenges of yet another day.

Monkey Woman

THE NATURAL SORCERESS

CHARMS AND SYMBOLS

Tarot card:	The Fool, which represents curiosity and initiative
Moon phase:	Waning
Celestial bodies:	Mercury
Herbs and plants:	Parsley, mint, lavender
Colors:	Yellow, gold, silver
Crystals and gemstones:	Citrine, quartz, yellow agate
Incense:	Lavender, almond
Lucky day:	Wednesday
Lucky numbers:	5, 14, 23
Ritual colors:	Yellow, gold
Ritual robes:	Satin, silks
Magickal symbols:	Monkeys, jesters, circles, cups, ravens, monkey's paws, thrones
Goddesses:	The sorceress, the mysterious, the hidden, the dark goddesses
Theme song:	"Bette Davis Eyes" by Kim Carnes

ASSOCIATED GODDESSES FOR THE MONKEY WOMAN

Circe: The Greek sorceress who tricked Ulysses into staying with her for many years. Circe had the power to turn people into animals, notably pigs. Often pictured with braided hair, she was seductive and powerful. She is said to have had the power to infuse wine with magick in order to trick her enemies.

Medea: The Greek goddess who was so awesome she was thought to be the origin of all healing. Her name means "Wise One." She was a great sorceress whose knowledge of magick was venerated.

Hecate: Witch goddess of magick and sorcery linked to the Greek trinity of goddesses, Hecate is regarded as the mother of all witches. She was linked to the underworld and the rites of magick, divination, and mediumship.

Hel: Nordic goddess of the underworld who was venerated throughout northern Europe for her great power and strength. Hel, like Hecate, was a part of the triple goddess in her maiden-mother-crone aspects. An encounter with a supernatural woman was referred to by the Danes as *hellig* or "hellish."

POSITIVE TRAITS

engaging	communicative
clever	emotional
intense	determined
enchanting	driven
adaptable	energetic
wily	warm
talkative	mischievous
commanding	curious

NEGATIVE TRAITS

draining	opportunistic
greedy	deceptive
noncommittal	tricky
insincere	bossy
loquacious	materialistic
overbearing	manipulative
controlling	illusionary
troublemaking	quarrelsome

fAMOUS MONKEY WOMEN

Jennifer Aniston · Jerry Hall · Carole Lombard · Bette Davis
Kylie Minogue · Lisa Marie Presley · Chelsea Clinton · Debbie Reynolds
Carrie Fisher · Elizabeth Taylor · Patricia Arquette · Peggy Lee
Lucy Liu · Ashley Judd · Rachel Griffiths · Lucy Lawless · Céline Dion

   ## MONKEY WOMAN'S NUMBER

1 Feisty and innovative, you like to be on your toes and keep others there too!

2 Gentle, entrancing, and searching for your soul mate, you love romance with a passion.

3 A literate, exciting Monkey, you're always thinking up new adventures and ideas.

4 Grounded and realistic, you have tremendous drive and energy.

5 Vivacious, temperamental, and electrifying. A high-voltage Monkey!

6 A family-minded Monkey. Extragenerous, but a bit of a softie. Be careful of con artists.

7 Independent, you can be somewhat standoffish. You have a razor-sharp mind.

8 Ambitious, demanding, and bound to make a lot of money, you're a Monkey with class.

9 You have great leadership qualities and enjoy the chase. You're dynamic and explosive, so watch that temper!

THE SORCERESS!

Whichever way you play the deck, the Monkey woman enjoys gambling and she usually comes up a winner. Smart, sophisticated, and fascinating, she can be a downright sorceress in her capacity to make things happen. No one else can be so good at planning her moves, and she just adores the thrill of the chase. Thoughtful and profound, the Monkey woman heads into life with gusto and panache!

The Monkey woman has a natural sparkle and pizzazz to her that is irresistible. However, engaging and friendly though she may appear to be, she always has a hidden agenda and a much more powerful energy than she shows. I have named her the "sorceress" because her energy invokes the illusion-creating capacity of the magickal goddesses like Medea and Hecate.

For this very reason, the Monkey woman often makes a superb and clever actor. She is able to create just the right illusion that blends both fantasy and reality. This is a very potent tool for success.

Take a look at some famous Monkey women and you'll immediately see the magick and power inherent in this sign. Monkey women Carole Lombard and Bette Davis were powerful screen goddesses of their time. Bette and Carole portrayed dark woman characters to perfection. Their performances illuminate the Monkey woman's extreme goal-seeking nature. The popular song "Bette Davis Eyes" pays tribute to the late sorceress's vibrant energy and charisma.

Monkey women often have very intense eyes. They reflect their powerful expression of thought with a quick brilliance that can be both striking and cutting. Just a glance from Bette, for example, says a million words. The brilliant violet of Elizabeth Taylor's eyes captured the hearts of countless men and husbands!

The Monkey woman's expression can also be playful, with more than a hint of Monkey mischievousness. Current-day actresses like Patricia Arquette and Rachel Griffiths possess these vibrant eyes.

Whether she appears as a green fairy or Marilyn Monroe, the Monkey woman has tremendous stamina and loves to test herself. Kylie Minogue, the "singing budgie," displays the Monkey woman's capacity for continual shape-changing over a succession of years and still continues to charm the jungle crowd. The Monkey woman is naturally self-assured with a healthy ego and a belief she can take on the world!

An intelligent sign, the Monkey woman likes to profit by others' mistakes. She usually tries a trick or two before she calculates her moves. She is not necessarily deceitful, but she certainly is capable of bending the truth if it will help her through an awkward predicament. Her motto might be "the end justifies the means." She needs to curb her opportunistic tendencies, however, otherwise she will exhaust herself.

The Monkey woman enchants many people, but her inherent desire to win at all costs may create some lifetime enemies. They will see her successful Monkey grip as a threat to their own piece of the jungle. For this reason, the Monkey woman would benefit from a deep study of the spiritual cause-and-effect law of karma. Also, a consideration of the goddess Circe would help her realize the power of destruction she is capable of and teach her to use it wisely. With her often very successful life, the Monkey woman may not reflect on the general rule "What goes around, comes around." She should realize her good luck and share a little fortune to deflect negative consequences.

The Monkey woman's passions are a major challenge area. Very few Monkey women find their true mate until later in life. As she is so ready to shape shift to please others, the Monkey lady rarely loses out on the initial pursuit. However she can waste time on potential losers!

Her main problem is in not knowing what partner to capture, as she needs to be sure of what she really wants. The Monkey lady can be fickle and somewhat commitment-shy partly because she is never without a wide circle of admirers. The Monkey woman requires an adoring and really passionate mate, not just someone who gets caught up in her enchantment.

The Monkey woman needs the challenge of worthwhile objects in her life or she may become bitter and vindictive. She can sometimes fall prey to her desires and moods, however, so she needs to watch extremes of emotions.

On the positive side, she has a rare magick that enables her to connect with many different types of people who are attracted to her whimsical and cheeky charm. She can be extremely successful in almost any field of life, and if she turns her magick to helping others, she can achieve fantastic victories.

MONKEY WOMAN AND LOVE

Entrapment should have been coined as the word to describe the Monkey woman in love. The Greek goddess Circe took a fancy to Ulysses and kept him on her island of enchantment for many years. Indeed, it took the intercession of the god Mercury to release him. In the same way, the wily Monkey knows how to turn on all the tricks to get her prey interested. She will enjoy this only so long as she does not end up chasing her own tail in the process.

The last of the great lovers, the Monkey woman can be a very passionate mate. She enjoys going after big prizes, but occasionally forgets to check if they are already promised. Monkey woman Elizabeth Taylor captured the husband of her Monkey sister Debbie Reynolds!

Love is a fairly overwhelming experience for the Monkey woman. She falls in love hard and may be more caught up in the process than actually knowing the person she appears so interested in. She can be fickle and discard her interests pretty rapidly. She can also veer toward the Dark Goddess energy of bitterness and vengefulness if she ends up playing the loser's role.

The Monkey woman needs a very involved partner who truly admires her. To keep her from jumping to another tree, her partner must be able to stimulate her both physically and mentally. Her partner's wit and intellect must match hers.

The Monkey woman's love energy is a major influence in her life. One challenge for her is to stop fussing and learn to trust in her relationships. Otherwise, she will jump from one to another in search of ever more excitement.

Another challenge for the Monkey woman is becoming so absorbed with her career that she neglects her mate. She would be best suited to an equally energetic partner who has his or her own life. Her active energy draws the weaker kind of partner, but this type seeks support from her and may pin her down to her detriment.

The Monkey woman can display flexibility when it comes to relationships. However, if she is not respected, her tougher side will emerge, as Mick Jagger found out with Monkey vamp Jerry Hall. The Monkey woman has quite a fiery side to her and can become very angry if deceived or hoodwinked in love.

Most Monkey women would rather move on than stay in an unhappy relationship. This trait, coupled with their strong need for companionship, means they are quite likely to have a number of short-term relationships. Finding their true

Monkey Woman and Compatibility

Monkey & Rat ♡	Can work if Monkey can avoid trying to rule over the Rat.
Monkey & Ox ♡♡♡	Monkey finds Ox a fragile partner. However, when Ox supports her, it can work out very well.
Monkey & Tiger ♡	Forget this one; two opposing signs that find fault with each other.
Monkey & Cat ♡♡	Monkey can help Cat develop, but Cat will need to overlook Monkey's tricks.
Monkey & Dragon ♡♡♡	Well suited. These two relate to each other deeply. The Dragon has the power to relate well to her.
Monkey & Snake ♡♡♡♡	Very compatible, yes! A pair of magickal mates.
Monkey & Horse ♡	No, Horse has a wandering soul. These two have difficulty finding common ground.
Monkey & Goat ♡	Goat can be devoted to Monkey's love. Monkey feels bored though.
Monkey & Monkey ♡♡♡	These two can twine around each other, finding major points of interest. A true match of mind and body!
Monkey & Rooster ♡♡♡	Lots of fun. The sex life will sparkle. Some sparks will fly though.
Monkey & Dog ♡♡♡	The Dog can be attentive, so a solid match is likely between these two.
Monkey & Pig ♡	No, this one is not recommended. Pig will come off second.

♡♡♡♡ = excellent   ♡♡♡ = good   ♡♡ = fair   ♡ = difficult

mate is a bit of a challenge for them as they view the world much like a monkey amongst a forest of trees. You never know what the next bough will hold, but Monkeys possess the stamina to keep going.

As a wife and mother the Monkey woman is well meaning, but sometimes she forgets to view her children and spouse as individuals. She will be a little too sure of herself at times and can lay down the law rather forcefully. The Monkey lady tends to dominate not so much from arrogance but simply because her quick temperament produces the fastest results. She can become impatient with those who do not always respond as fast as her. She needs to sit on the back fence occasionally and listen more to the thoughts of others, no matter how irritatingly slow they appear compared to her own lightning-quick processes. Monkey women can steer a happy family unit when she steers *with* them, not at them.

MONKEY WOMAN AND HEALTH

This area has to be watched as the Monkey woman always feels she is strong! Usually she likes to party, smoke, and drink, which, if not tempered, may cause long-term health issues. Regular exercise and even relatively strenuous activities such as horse riding or squash are generally good for her physique and will entertain her mentally as well as match her quick movements.

The Monkey woman generally has great resilience and can live to a ripe old age with a temperate lifestyle. She needs to avoid taking undue risks and eat foods that cleanse her liver and pancreas. Deep-breathing exercises are also good for her as she may suffer hay fever or allergies and would benefit from lots of fresh air.

Normally quite a survivor, the Monkey woman weathers emotional storms with competence. Her nerves may need soothing, however, as she tends to repress her feelings too much. Nervous Monkey women should practice meditation.

MONKEY WOMAN AND FINANCES

The Monkey woman can make a million and lose it again if she doesn't learn to be more discerning in business dealings. She is normally gifted, clever, and a good earner, but should invest in safe ventures like property. She can do very well in self-employment, and she is often met with financial luck when she travels. Many fortunate Monkeys marry wealthy partners.

MONKEY WOMAN AS A CHILD

This is a wind-you-around-my-fingers child capable of weaving an unforgettable spell. The Monkey child is very ambitious and conscious of peer pressure. She wants to stand out in the crowd and be noticed by everyone. She loves creative enterprises and may be a little businesswoman at an early age. Sometimes impetuous and a bit hot-tempered, she enjoys all manner of sport and play.

As an adolescent, the Monkey may be difficult to reason with. It is a good idea not to be overdisciplinary, as this will only cause her to rebel further. Involving this one in your decisions and day-to-day plans will give her a sense of appreciation and satisfy her need to be noticed. She can be easily charmed with play and attention.

MONKEY WOMAN AND CAREER

The Monkey woman's career ideally should be stimulating and even a little risky; she will thrive on challenging tasks. When Monkey woman Debbie Reynolds hit a low period in her life and lost all her money, she reinvented herself by turning her talents to running a hotel.

The Monkey woman is able to turn her hand to a myriad of activities and have several going on at one time. Communication areas are natural for her, especially fields like writing, media, and the arts. She would also do well in fast-paced jobs like public relations, investigation, and marketing. Large organizations suit her, but only if she wins the leading role.

Running her own establishment such as a hotel or restaurant would also suit the Monkey woman. This type of work would give her plenty of scope to both take charge and exert a lot of energy. She does not suit work that is oversupervised or has no promotional prospect, as she wants to be in control and on the move.

MONKEY WOMAN IN THE TWENTY-FIRST CENTURY

The Monkey woman is the great innovator and will adapt well to the pressure of life that surrounds us in the twenty-first century. She has the ability to be quite a leader in a number of fields. We should see some fine Monkey woman writers, communicators, and actors emerge as we enter the period when children who were born when Pluto was in Scorpio (1984–1995) begin to grow up and probe life's depths. At this time, artists and communicators born under the Monkey's sign will prosper. The Monkey woman will also enter politics and Monkey prime ministers and presidents may well come to the fore.

MONKEY WOMAN AND SPIRITUALITY

The monkey as a sacred animal has long been revered in many cultures as a spiritual symbol of occult power. Interestingly, most Monkey women of my acquaintance are very curious about the spiritual world. This sign is open to experimentation, and she does not necessarily follow any set religious pattern. Instead, she enjoys discussions on all aspects of the otherworld and loves to increase her knowledge.

The Monkey woman can gain important life lessons from the study of the goddesses like Circe, the Greek underworld sorceress, healer, and witch. Circe was known for her exceptional knowledge and powerful craft. As the Monkey lady develops and nurtures her spiritual side, she will come to terms with a lot of the challenges life has given her.

As with all Dark Goddesses, the Monkey woman has the power to heal and the wisdom to let go of negative emotions. Knowing and respecting her divine self leads her to empowerment on every level.

RITUAL WORK FOR THE MONKEY WOMAN

INVOKING CIRCE FOR SPECIAL PETITIONS

Ritual Tools
- One red and one yellow ribbon
- A photograph album filled with favorite shots
- Meditative music to be played during the ritual
- One stick each of frankincense and myrrh incense
- A small hand-held mirror
- One small crystal bowl
- A glass of wine

Ritual Time
Just before or at the time of the new moon.

Place all the items listed above on your altar. The photograph album and mirror should be placed together. Put a drop of red wine in the crystal bowl to offer the goddess.

First relax by listening to the music. Move to its beat if you feel so inclined. Light the incense and candles and visualize energy in the form of a circle of golden light around you. Invoke the goddess Circe as follows:

> "Oh great goddess Circe, I invite with respect your magickal power and energy to assist me in my petitions. [*State petitions here.*] I recognize my own magickal power to enchant and emulate, however, I seek to use my magick for higher good! I am grateful for my quick wit and intelligence and wish to give my gift to the world. Help me to see my life path clearly and to utilize the gifts I have been blessed with to best serve my own karma and give joy to my sisters and brothers."

Open your photo album to a treasured moment and thank the goddess for your gifts. Wind the yellow and red ribbons together to symbolize the interweaving of your love with those you hold dear. If you are a single woman, you may like to visualize the interweaving as your love aura reaching out to your soul mate, or the strengthening of your own energy with that of the goddess.

Make a toast to the goddess with the wine. Then leave the yellow and red ribbons on the altar for a lunar month, and keep your mirror in your handbag or private space to remind you of the power of self-knowledge. Conclude the ritual by snuffing out the candles and incense.

INVOKING HECATE FOR LOVE

Ritual Tools
· Picture or effigy of a monkey
· A cup of red wine or another red-colored drink
· One red candle
· Lavender incense
· A white rose

Ritual Time
New moon in Taurus or Libra.

Prepare your altar with the tools above in a favorite spot in your house. Light the incense and candle and place the monkey symbol between the two. Sit and close your eyes. Breathe deeply in through your mouth and slowly release out through your nose. Do this three or four times until you feel all your body become relaxed and still.

Now invoke the goddess Hecate by chanting the following:

"Goddess of magick and sorcery, I honor your positive strength. I am in need of love [*new or to renew*] and I ask for a sincere mate who understands my complexities."

Visualize your body surrounded by golden rays swirling in slow, gentle circle patterns around you. See one strong ray emanate from the center of your chest out toward the monkey symbol on the altar and beyond. It reaches to a shadow of your mate waiting on the other side of the altar.

Visualize your mate sitting on the other side of this altar as a mirror reflection; see this person's light also touching you. Feel the warmth of your mate's rays and know that this spiritual connection will bring you together.

Now toast to your mate spirit with a sip of the drink. In your mind see him or her partake of the drink from the same cup. Your hands overlap as your mate holds the cup to his or her lips. Then sprinkle some of the liquid over the white rose and dedicate this to the goddess.

Snuff out your candle and conclude your ritual. Leave the petals as they fall on the altar. Each time you perform this meditation, collect the fallen petals and keep them in a bowl near where you sleep and dream.

MEDITATION FOR CALM AND FOCUSING

Close your eyes and see yourself in a grand library. You are sitting in a comfortable armchair in front of a cozy fire reading your favorite book. You are surrounded by polished wood bookcases full of books and special ornaments. Among these ornaments are many likenesses of monkeys of all kinds. This is your personal totem animal.

There is an old oak table in front of you covered with a gold tablecloth. An antique vase full of yellow carnations sits on the table next to a glass of red berry juice in a pewter goblet. Now and then you take a sip from the cup, savoring its sweet taste.

You are content and at ease in this special place. It contains not only your favorite books, but also your private journals, within which you have recorded special personal memories. As you continue to read, you reflect on the power of words to heal when used in a positive manner. You acknowledge this gift in yourself. You take time to remember any writers who have affected you profoundly.

There is a movement near you and you are momentarily startled to hear a tapping on the library window. You close your book, rise, and walk to the window. Outside is a magnificent black raven!

You have no fear of this creature because he looks at you so knowingly. It is clear to you that he has a special message for you. You unlock the window catch and let him in. His wings brush your shoulder as he flies gently by you into the room.

He seems to have something in his beak. As you examine it more closely, you see it is a pendant of yellow citrine quartz crystal attached to a gold chain. The raven drops it at your feet and perches himself on the table.

Bending to pick it up, you feel strangely drawn to the pendant's aura. You place it around your neck. The raven speaks to you with a low, deep voice. He says, "Take the wisdom and power you need from within yourself. Be responsible for your own happiness. This pendant represents your powerful intellect."

You feel very happy you have connected with this special guide. You settle yourself back in the armchair with your raven at your side. You take a few moments to meditate on your life at present and resolve to have a positive attitude. Understand that your raven is always with you to act as your advisor.

When you are ready, slowly open your eyes. Write down or record any insights you received while meditating. Your library will always be there when you wish to return. When you are able to, you may like to obtain a piece of citrine quartz to remind you of your vision and its meaning.

Snake Woman

THE NATURAL SIREN

CHARMS AND SYMBOLS

Tarot card: The Lovers, which represents the choice between the sexes and the soul

Moon phase: New

Celestial bodies: Venus, Pluto

Herbs and plants: Elder, valerian, blackberry

Colors: Blues, greens, bright pinks

Crystals and gemstones: Snakeskin jasper, diamond

Incense: Rose, vanilla, violet

Lucky day: Friday

Lucky numbers: 6, 24, 33

Ritual colors: Green, blue

Ritual robes: Fur, or fake fur, animal prints (especially snakeskin print), satin, velvet

Magickal symbols: Snakes, the caduceus, circles, spiders, the scarab

Goddesses: Seducers, sirens, the dark goddesses, regenerative goddesses

Theme song: "Sexual Healing" by Marvin Gaye

ASSOCIATED GODDESSES FOR THE SNAKE WOMAN

Lakshmi: Beautiful, desirable Hindu goddess associated with qualities similar to Venus and Aphrodite. She was the partner of Vishnu, the great god of creation.

Meretseger: Cobra goddess of ancient Egypt. Meretseger is said to be both dangerous and merciful. She is also believed to have the power to heal or destroy.

Medusa: Greek goddess with the power to turn men to stone. Medusa was depicted with snakes on her head instead of hair. She was the serpent goddess of the Libyan Amazons and ancient myth aligns her with the destroyer aspect of the Triple Goddess of Libya.

Coatlicue: Aztec earth mother and serpent lady who wore a skirt of snakes associated with the deepest aspects of creation. The Aztecs designated her as an astrological sign. She was said to be the mother of the earth, moon, and stars.

POSITIVE TRAITS

natural	intuitive
discreet	astute
artistic	subtle
sexual	alluring
imaginative	artistic
mystical	nostalgic
amusing	creative
stylish	perceptive
profound	wise
intense	intellectual

NEGATIVE TRAITS

fussy	deceitful
superficial	vain
secretive	promiscuous
status-seeking	materialistic
cutting	snobby
illogical	depressed
ungrounded	lazy
unfocused	calculating
slow-moving	escapist
addictive	fanatical

fAMOUS SNAKE WOMEN

Ann-Margret · Kim Basinger · Queen Elizabeth I · Liv Tyler
Sarah Michelle Gellar · Sarah Jessica Parker · Grace Kelly · Christie Brinkley
Jacqueline Kennedy · Elizabeth Hurley · Kate Capshaw · Gillian Anderson
Oprah Winfrey · Audrey Hepburn · Susan Seddon Boulet · Anne Rice
J. K. Rowling · Mary Shelley · Greta Garbo · Amy Irving · Linda McCartney

SNAKE WOMAN'S NUMBER

1 An independent Snake, you could do well in the political arena. You have a certain sense of purpose.

2 You seek true soul-mate energy and need to be particularly careful of your escapist side. Temper the emotions!

3 You are a great communicator and love to delve deeply. A great investigator Snake

4 You put a great deal of your passion into practical matters.

5 Great for a thespian Snake and would-be Shakespeare. You are creative, ingenious, and clever.

6 Love is all-consuming for you. Watch obsessions and compulsions.

7 Psychic, psychic, psychic! You do have real insight, so use it!

8 You are businesslike and serious with a flair for managing others.

9 Insightful and clever, you could be a very intellectual Snake. Potential leader!

THE SIREN!

One look at the brief list of famous Snake women in history displays a clear picture of great beauties. They are stylish trend-setters attentive to the energy of the love goddess in their appearance and psyche. Snake woman Queen Elizabeth I was a style queen to such an extent that the whole age she ruled over was named after her! You can't really get to be more of a trend-setter than that, can you?

Sinuous, seductive, and natural sirens, Snake women both enchant and seduce us. We are enthralled by their beauty and sense of style, fascinated with the feminine mystery, and curious as to exactly how they put it all together. One thing is for sure: it works!

This woman combines the energies of both the erotic love goddess and the Dark Goddess in equal proportions. This duality explains the high proportion of Snake women who achieve celebrity status. Snake women are never simple to understand. They are complex, usually very intelligent, curious, and great thinkers.

The Snake woman is an extraordinary example of female alluring energy at its most concentrated. She spends great amounts of time calculating how to please and usually succeeds very well. Modern fashion icons like Liv Tyler and Sarah Jessica Parker are Snakes.

Watch out if you have a close Snake girlfriend! Pretty soon your partner will be noticing how she does her hair or the color of her eyes. People can't help but notice her, even if she has no intention of "capturing" them. Seduction is as natural to her as breathing and is a primary part of her personality.

The Snake woman is seldom questioning of her sexual attraction and is usually not shy about it. As a teenager she will experiment with a few way-out exotic styles and may spend some time working out which one really gets the best attention. It is not unusual for younger Snakes to be attracted to piercing their nose or other parts of their body or even getting an appropriate tattoo done. The Snake woman enjoys admiration and loves to be seen. It is this quality that makes her so elegant in her later life, and gives her her keen artistic eye for beauty.

Alluring and seductive, Elizabeth I was fascinated with her appearance and is said to have owned over two thousand dresses! Her love of beauty, fashion, and style was legendary. She was said to be a woman of keen intellect and appraisal smart enough to have survived an extremely barbaric age. She was also secretive and calculating, using both qualities to her advantage.

The Snake woman calculates to please with a naturally good head start. She is blessed with natural beauty and the drawing power of Venus, and she makes the most of what nature has given her.

She also has the power of the mystical goddess inherent within her. She is naturally intuitive to the point of psychic ability. The Snake woman can be extremely perceptive and usually is of a profound mindset. When she becomes out of touch with her spiritual side, however, the Snake woman is often drawn to escapism—and sometimes addiction. She needs to find the spiritual part of herself if she is to maintain her balance and stay grounded in life.

Being able to hypnotize so many potential partners is fascinating, but getting the real soul match is as much a challenge for the Snake woman as for anyone else. Too many seductions and disappointments after the thrill of the chase leave her weary of it all. Deep down she is truly seeking a total mind-body-spirit connection with a special partner. Indeed, this aspect of life can be more difficult for her because underneath she is so fussy about those she allows to be really close to her. The Snake woman may have many lovers, but usually she only has one or two great loves. Her heart is quite reserved and her tastes exacting.

Snake woman Elizabeth I never married, preferring to keep her freedom. She could not find a balance between power and love. History tells us that although she had plenty of admirers of her beauty and style, Elizabeth did not have many true loves. Her heart was captured by only a small handful of men, perhaps the Lord of Essex amongst them.

Another problem the Snake woman faces is frightening people with her intensity and passion. She lives so much in the "snake" coil that she sometimes forgets to uncoil occasionally and become more flexible to life. On the other hand, although she is capable of great achievements, the Snake woman can suffer from periods of indolence, and even laziness, which prevent her from reaching her creative and personal goals. If she does master her creative energy, the Snake woman can become a great artist, creator, and innovator.

The Snake lady also has innate healing capacities. Snake and great twentieth-century beauty Audrey Hepburn worked tirelessly for starving children, bringing out the inner beauty of the Snake. Oprah Winfrey also has tapped into this inner reserve by bringing positive and helpful images to the masses. Her Snake sisters Anne Rice and J. K. Rowling delve into the magickal and the unseen with their hugely successful writing.

It is usually very helpful for the Snake woman to study the meaning of the kundalini energy to which she is very closely related. Having knowledge of its power and regenerative abilities will help her make more informed choices in her life.

SNAKE WOMAN AND LOVE

We can see where this woman stands out in the love stakes. She is magnetic, sexual, and alluring, often beautiful, and memorable. Her challenges lie in her passions becoming too obsessive, particularly where her love objects are concerned. She can emotionally suffocate them.

The Snake woman must be aware of love becoming an obsession to seduce for her, without firstly, knowing what she is getting, and secondly, destroying it once she has it. Many Snakes of my acquaintance are puzzled and hurt when a love match does not work out after they invest so much seductive energy into it. Two things stand in the way of the Snake finding true love and happiness: lack of discernment and overpossessiveness.

The Snake woman takes a while to work out what she is really searching for. Because she is magnetic and extremely feminine, she may attract superficial men who look at their partner as a trophy rather than a person. The Snake woman, because of her innate sexual drawing power, often attracts highly sexed men who find it difficult to be satisfied with just one woman or who may have problems committing.

As one of her innate capacities is the developing of wisdom, the Snake woman can achieve greater emotional happiness if she begins to discern what sort of partner she is attracting and what she really wants. If she dresses or acts like a siren, she will call all manner of sailors toward her. Holding back a little is a wise move for our Snake lady. This gives her time to work out the real person, not just the acquaintance.

Deep down the Snake woman needs a devoted, almost doting partner. What she often partners with are well-heeled playboys who ultimately do not give her much emotional sustenance. She must also beware the tendency to overpossess her mate.

Snake Woman and Compatibility

Snake & Rat
♡♡

Although a strong attraction exists, these two are very complex and deep.

Snake & Ox
♡

Ox is very strong, but may be too stubborn for the Snake. Snake feels a lack of passion in the Ox.

Snake & Tiger
♡

Tiger is too manipulative and Snake is too touchy.

Snake & Cat
♡♡♡

Can work, but the Cat mate is touchy and Snake wants passion, not fuss.

Snake & Dragon
♡♡♡

Can be both long-lasting and incredibly exciting. Yes!

Snake & Snake
♡♡♡♡

Two coiled ones can be very passionate. They study the deeper aspects of life.

Snake & Horse
♡

No, Horse is too freedom-loving; Snake will be frustrated.

Snake & Goat
♡♡

The gentleness of the Goat appeals to the Snake, so union can be sweet and potentially long-lasting.

Snake & Monkey
♡♡♡♡

This one is a powerful match of a siren and a sorcerer. Magick abounds!

Snake & Rooster
♡♡

Yes, these two have a fighting chance. The Rooster can be too fiery for the sinuous Snake though.

Snake & Dog
♡♡

Both are intense and loyal; a promising match. Dog will find Snake sexy.

Snake & Pig
♡

These two are so attracted to each other, but Pig is not really Snake's cup of tea.

♡♡♡♡ – excellent   ♡♡♡ – good   ♡♡ – fair   ♡ = difficult

As a wife, the Snake woman is creative and clever. She is able to help her mate's ambitions in many ways. As a mother, she will be possessive and needs to learn to detach herself from her offspring at times. The Snake woman holds very high standards for her loved ones and may not always express her real feelings, which can lead to confusion.

Yet the Snake woman does have the capacity to shed her skin in love as in everything else. She can merely make up her mind to attain better relationships once she has realized her self. The Snake lady has the capacity to form amazingly deep bonds.

SNAKE WOMAN AND HEALTH

Health can be a variable for the Snake woman, who tends to well and truly burn the candle at both ends. She loves to be the center of attention, and pays great attention to detail and appearance, sometimes to her detriment. Excessive dieting, too many late nights, or the use of substances like nicotine or other pick-me-ups will inevitably affect her nervous system. Stomach and liver organs could be damaged with years of excessive use or abuse. In order to achieve longevity, the Snake lady should begin to temper her bad habits at an early age and eat sensible, healthy food at regular intervals. Regular and sustained exercise, meditation, and yoga are all very beneficial for her. She should quit smoking, limit overexertion, and limit alcohol intake. Tai chi and other related gentle movement exercises best match her natural snakelike rhythm and energy.

SNAKE WOMAN AND FINANCES

The Snake woman tends to be a good spender, loving luxury items and designer labels. She has a great eye for antiques and objects of art. She usually earns a sufficient income to maintain this, but should be careful of being a slave to image. She usually marries well and will happily spend her partner's money. The Snake woman needs to plan her spending so savings will grow easily from a usually good income. Snakes are very seldom poor.

SNAKE WOMAN AS A CHILD

The Snake woman is enchanting, wise, and strong-minded as a child. She devours everything mentally and demands to increase her knowledge. She is usually curious and charming, often taking a dominant role amongst her siblings. She will be attracted to creative, fun activities and have a keen intellect.

The sign of the Snake is connected to death and rebirth. Because of this, there may have been some danger to the mother's life at the birth of her Snake child. The Snake child's entry will have been linked to a major transformation in the mother's own life cycle.

The Snake child normally will be rebellious as a teenager and will benefit from a strong, sound education, including about the dangers of drug use. Her creative energy will peak as an adolescent, so her parents would be wise to channel this into something positive. Her sexual curiosity will also be powerful, so again she needs to be given proper education in this area.

SNAKE WOMAN AND CAREER

The Snake woman loves Venusian-ruled career areas like the creative arts, acting, art appreciation, beautician, modeling, and writing. It's no coincidence that one finds so many Snakes in the acting world!

Dancing, music, and all creative arts attract the Snake woman. She can also succeed in health-related careers such as nursing or medicine. Snakes possess a confirmed intellect and may be drawn to politics and community leadership roles. The worst career choices for the Snake lady would be boring or monotonous positions that restrict her freedom to explore, as she needs challenge.

SNAKE WOMAN IN THE TWENTY-FIRST CENTURY

The Snake woman will be drawn to conquer fields in the twenty-first century and may be found at the forefront of new medical and technological changes. She will be needed in the development of women in politics as well.

If she moves from seducing to mastering her power, the Snake can be one of the most successful of the animal signs. At this point in time, she can take her place in major leadership roles where her creativity and profound mind can be utilized for the good of others.

SNAKE WOMAN AND SPIRITUALITY

Like her natural witch cousin the Rat, the Snake woman relates to the powerful energies of the Dark Goddess. She possesses some of the subterranean energy of the underworld and needs to learn to integrate this into her everyday life.

In her spiritual self, the Snake has a powerful connection to healing, death, rebirth, and the spirit world. As such she can be a powerful medium. She is aware of the other spheres around us and is linked to the spirit in a profound way.

The Snake may become a little afraid of her intuitive side and may seek to repress it. Like the Rat, she needs to accept and be comfortable with this natural connection. Once the Snake woman does connect with spirituality, she is capable of mastering remarkable insights into human nature, as did author Mary Shelley in her epic tale of destruction and creation, *Frankenstein*.

It is a strange twist of their nature that many Snakes deny their interest in the hidden and the mysterious, even though they are secretly fascinated by this sphere of existence. It is almost as if they find it difficult to integrate their two energies of the upperworld self and the hidden self lying just below their shedding skin. The Snake needs to shed her outer self to awaken the Snake spirit underneath.

The Snake woman will learn how her sexual being connects to the greater life force energy, and take this side of her to a deeper level, if she is to make sense of many aspects of her complex life. If she affords herself a chance to learn about the life energies of the sexual Goddess, she will understand that her spirituality and her sexuality can be balanced to create a natural power. This balancing of her extreme powers is one of her greatest challenges.

I have noted her connection to the goddesses like Medusa who turned men to stone to remind the Snake woman about her destructive side as well. She has the capability to turn her kundalini power one way or the other. The following magickal rituals are specially designed for the Snake woman's expression.

RITUAL WORK FOR THE SNAKE WOMAN

INVOKING COATLICUE FOR SPECIAL PETITIONS

Ritual Tools
· A piece of jewelry such as a necklace
· A handful of red stones
· Four green candles
· A snake charm or ornament
· One stick of rose incense
· A skirt or petticoat especially dedicated to the ritual

Ritual Time
New moon, ideally in or near Scorpio.

Prepare your altar by arranging the red stones in the shape of a snake. Place two candles on the right and left sides of the altar. Place the snake charm directly in front of you on the altar.

Don the ritual skirt or undergarment and jewelry. Light the candles, burn the incense, and meditate quietly. As you do, visualize the point at the base of your spine, which is the kundalini point in the body.

Invoke the goddess Coatlicue as follows:

"Oh honored and revered goddess, I call on your great power and fertility. I honor you and respect the life force within myself. Help me to work my magick toward the following: [*state your aims here*]. Protect me and balance my life."

Snuff out the candles and incense, and as you do this, visualize the goddess. Dedicate the jewelry piece to the goddess and wear it in honor of her.

INVOKING LAKSHMI FOR LOVE AND ATTRACTION

Ritual Tools

· A small mirror
· Four red candles
· One stick each of rose and vanilla incense
· Red ritual robes
· Snakeskin jasper
· Picture or representation of Lakshmi

Ritual Time

Full moon in Taurus or Libra.

On your altar, arrange your ritual tools. Burn the candles and incense. Invoke the goddess as follows:

> "Great goddess Lakshmi, I realize your immense beauty and honor your powers. Help me to find the true mate of my soul who perceives my beauty within. I honor and respect my sexuality and desirability and I request a partner who venerates the goddess within me. Bring me romance, love, and companionship."

Dedicate the mirror, jasper, and representation of Lakshmi to the goddess and then snuff out the candles and incense.

MEDITATION FOR INNER CALM AND STRENGTH

Close your eyes and imagine standing in a large, open field. Surrounding you is a series of mirrors twelve feet high and six feet across held in deep gold frames. You look at each mirror, but all you see is the reflection of the field stretching out ahead of you—green grass and blue sky.

Now look again. As you look at the first mirror you choose, see yourself as a little girl playing with a toy you can recall from your childhood. Remember what that toy felt like, looked like, and smelled like. Now look at the second mirror. There you are as a young girl. See yourself somewhere where you had to be strong. Was it at school standing up to bullies? Was it at a social event where you had to say something you found difficult to do? Was it an argument with your parents or siblings? Congratulate yourself on being strong enough to have this now as a memory.

Now look at the third mirror, where you see yourself now. What do you look like? See not just your outer body, but see the soul within. Are you happy with what you see? If not, today is the time to start changing that reflection into what you want it to be. Look around you. There are many more mirrors; each holds a different memory and each one is a reflection of your journey so far. But look again: there are even more mirrors and they are blank, yet to be filled with a part of your experience. Concentrate on one of these mirrors and look into it. See now what you want to make of yourself and believe that you can do it.

Now open your eyes and breathe deeply. You can reinvent yourself over and over again. There is no limit to what you can achieve and change in yourself. Remember, it is the inner self that reflects your beauty, and that is the mirror you hold up unconsciously for the world to see. Only those who look beyond the surface can see the true beauty within.

PART VI

Goddess Types
& Relationships

Goddess Signs and Karma

Every year, my work brings me into contact with literally hundreds of women seeking spiritual counseling and life coaching. My clients come from all walks of life, including businesspeople, celebrities, politicians, health-care workers, and many others from all sorts of backgrounds, ages, and ethnic groups. They are at various stages in their lives. Some are new mothers, others are married, single, divorced, or widowed, or in between relationships actively seeking a mate. They all have a quest in common though: a desire for inner knowledge to help them take charge of their lives. Many seek a deeper understanding of their pathway in life, and this naturally leads them to explore their spirituality.

In my readings, I usually incorporate astrology, birth patterns, tarot, and palmistry to gain a well-rounded perspective of the direction of my client's lives. From the study of countless individual cases, I have uncovered an amazing pattern of astrology and karma patterns. I have compared sessions for modern women with women of an earlier generation and quite consistently found striking differences in their readings. These may include types and timing of major life experiences, timing of relationships, and even life spans.

Many years ago, I began to see a pattern of longer and longer life energies on many of the palms I read. There has been much written recently regarding the longer life expectation rates for the human race, with one prediction of an average life span of 100–120 or more years. This corresponds with the trends I began seeing on the hands years ago.

The other startling pattern I have observed is the trend toward much later life partnerships and connections. From what I have seen, many women's major life partners will not come into their lives until they are well into their thirties or forties. This trend is also coupled with signs of multiple partners, as opposed to spending life with one love alone. This is a very different reading from earlier generations, which tend to show a much earlier life partner connection and/or a strong, single love bond for women. The trend toward later life partners is already being reflected in the increasing numbers of single people in their twenties and thirties and even forties and fifties, with many women coming out of early relationships and spending quite a lot of time just being single, with or without children.

As a race, we evolve through different periods of biology, history, and geography. I personally believe we also evolve spiritually toward soul evolution through several lives. Although much has been written about how to find your perfect partner and how to conjure up the lover of your dreams through spells, I believe we need to take a look at our spiritual path and the ever-increasing life span to change the way we see our relationships. Learning about our spirit's potential is the true purpose of our relationships, not emotional fulfillment alone.

I believe partnerships ultimately depend on where you are at spiritually and what you will personally achieve and give as a result of a relationship. It may well be that you do not need a partner at very specific times in your life. I hope this book will help you realize that being single can be an empowering tool for self-fulfillment even in—or indeed, in spite of—a society that tends to dwell on and promote the "twosome" philosophy.

My work has convinced me that spiritually—and consequently, socially—we are evolving toward a new race of men and women who reflect the true concept of the Aquarian Age. Over the following few years, individuals will accelerate in their soul evolution. Concepts of restrictions or limitations held by earlier generations will no longer apply. There will be a new liberation of spirit that humans will access and want to reach.

Women will discover again their intrinsic goddess power and begin to move away from the concept of needing a partner to be their official "other half." Instead, they will realize that true spirituality acknowledges the potential to find divinity and wholeness within one's own soul. We will begin to understand that partnerships in the future will be more of a choice than an assumed way of life.

True, it is a choice that many take now. In the future, however, society will also begin to move away from the stereotypic expectations present today such as what time a partner should ideally come into your life, what age you should be settled down at, what age your partner should be, and what physical and material status you should both be aiming for. Today's materialistic forces increase "karmic bondage" between individuals in a way that tends to retard personal evolution. A move away from these societal pressures will be seen as positive in freeing up time and energy for spiritual clarity and development. "Soul" relationships that truly represent connections between people on a spiritual and heartfelt level, rather than on a primarily physical and emotional one, will become more prevalent as souls begin to work through their karmic or past-life lessons. Differing evolving needs for self-knowledge will move people toward higher levels of consciousness.

I believe many current relationships are based primarily on karmic bonds; that is, people learning and evolving through pretty tough life lessons that are being worked through in their present lives together. Within the next decade or so, many individuals will come out of these karmic relationships ready to experience a soul connection, where there is true mutual growth and enjoyment.

The term *soul mate* has been used and abused over the last twenty or so years, leaving its actual meaning blurred. A soul mate is not necessarily someone you fall madly in love with and live with happily ever after. It can also be someone you relate to on a spiritual level, and this can result in many different types of relationships, *including* those in which you need to sort out karmic bonds and difficulties.

Long-lasting and mutually beneficial relationships will take place for many people more commonly in the later part of their lives. This will correspond to a period when most individuals have already dealt with their "learning relationships" in earlier years.

I do not believe there is an easy way to develop spirituality. We do learn, evolve, and become stronger beings through suffering, pain, and difficulties. Overcoming challenges in our lives, whether in our personal relationships or our physical circumstances, makes us superior people to what we previously were. However, none of this takes away from the need to be positive in our choices or our capacity to love and grow.

For the modern woman, accepting her divine life-affirming energies and dealing with the power of her emotions will lead to a new dawn. No one pretends that this is going to be an easy path, but we can take measures to deal with the challenge positively. Openness to self-knowledge, taking responsibility for your soul's growth and its destiny, and refusing to be brainwashed by rapidly outdated ideas will help the magick truly happen! Willingness to bring the spiritual into one's life is becoming increasingly important in a world fraught with so much tension and uncertainty.

In the following pages, I discuss the likely karmic pathways your relationships will take, including the partnerships that are most positive. The following sections deal with your divine energy, which comes from an understanding of the strengths and weaknesses of your Goddess Sign.

Meditations

In the following sections, I have included meditations that you may like to practice along with your ritual work. Meditation is highly beneficial for de-stressing and focusing your thoughts.

Meditations and ritual work are best suited to a private "temple" where you can retreat from the demands and pressures of everyday life. Set aside a special place, either indoors or out, and practice your affirmations and meditations there. Remember, your guides are always with you. Invite them into your space whenever you feel the need.

Use the following invocation to call on the deity or spirit of your choice for protection at the beginning of meditations and rituals:

> "[*Spirit's name and/or description*], seal my space and aura, allowing only the positive flow of energy in my work."

These meditations, however, can also be adapted for groups of women working together. For example, where there are a number of different Goddess Signs, you may wish to add energy to each other's rituals by performing specific meditations in a private setting. Phases of the moon suitable for karmic meditations are when the moon is waning, or at least a week after the full moon.

If you are all performing as a group, honor all the energies present (e.g., the Sun Goddess, Moon Goddess, and so on) and a representative goddess from the ones covered under your signs. Spend some time meditating on each goddess energy present, and set up an altar in honor of each one. You may wish to think of what the particular energies of the goddesses represent to you at this stage in your personal journey and why you may have been drawn to look at them further at this time.

Perform your meditations, focusing on each person and her karmic journey. Give each person your energy as she performs her karmic meditation. Afterwards, do some divination or chanting to relax and celebrate. Your connection with the goddess should be joyful no matter what karmic issues are present.

DARK GODDESS RELATIONSHIPS AND KARMA

Dark Goddess women return to learn about the energies of the hidden and the underworld and deal with deep emotional issues and lessons. They also have the potential to heal and relieve the suffering of others.

Their gifts of knowledge can and do help others. As they evolve and grow, Dark Goddess women often form intimate connections with underworld-type partners. These types of mates are those dealing with their private demons and inner temptations.

As Dark Goddess women become more self-aware, they will notice a pattern to their relationships. They will experience the same types of issues over and over. If they assimilate into future practice what they have intuitively learned, they will better fulfill their life journey and stabilize their relationships.

Dark Goddess women writers like Charlotte Brontë and Margaret Mitchell portray their heroines as going through "dark-nights-of-the-soul" journeys. Their heroes are men who had also passed through the darkness and emerged with greater humanity and compassion, as depicted by the characters of Mr. Rochester in *Jane Eyre* and Rhett Butler in *Gone with the Wind*. In both novels, the writers chose to portray men filled with torment and fighting inner demons as the "hero" instead of the more conventional and well-balanced stereotype. In *Jane Eyre*, Jane realizes the complex Mr. Rochester is her soul mate, while in *Gone with the Wind*, Scarlett discovers, perhaps too late, her true affinity with the unconventional Rhett.

Karmically, Dark Goddess women attract partners who are in the grip of facing the underworld either in the form of compulsiveness, obsessional tendencies, or dark moods. They may also have the same tendencies within themselves. Dark Goddess women must learn to discern the difference between those souls who are in the process of still undertaking this journey and those who have moved on from this experience.

Their true partner is not the intoxicating, dangerous person who seems obsessed with their energy, but the mature, compassionate person who has embraced his or her dark side and is now ready to share life with someone else. Warning signals for these women are mates who are addictive, facing financial or personal crisis, obsessed with the past, abusive or escapist, ambivalent, or noncommittal. They will often find themselves powerfully attracted to such types for the learning they will impart, although significant pain will be involved. When they are ready to move on to a more mature type of partnership, however, Dark Goddess women should visualize themselves with mature, wise mates.

Evolving Meditation for Dark Goddess Women

Your vision journey is from the underworld to the upperworld.

Visualize some of your prior relationships, especially those that represented a definite underworld current. See a particular past mate in front of you. Release and surrender any lingering feelings of hurt or disappointment you may have been holding as your energies generate powerful feelings. Congratulate yourself for surviving the challenge, forgive your prior partner, and center yourself in *your strength.*

Picture yourself having the fortitude to dive into a deep, dark pool, and then swim effortlessly to the surface. As you do this, focus on the beauty of life that is often hidden under the ground and needs effort and courage to find. Visualize the magnificence and unbelievable diversity of all the creatures that live in harmony in the depths of the seas, some of which we have not even seen.

Recite to yourself the following:

> "I acknowledge my spiritual depths and power. I do not fear the underworld as my soul has received mastery over it. I choose to give my gifts back to the world."

Then visualize yourself surrounded in your own bright energy, and raise yourself with ease out of the pool and back onto the firm ground again. See yourself empowered with new and exciting knowledge.

In the distance you perceive a light. It is an easy-flowing energy that represents your new relationship or your renewed present relationship. Approach this light feeling refreshed and invigorated. Allow the light to approach you. Within this light energy is the mature wise soul who is waiting to connect to your mature self. Welcome this and expect to see the new person manifest in your life.

SUN GODDESS RELATIONSHIPS AND KARMA

Sun Goddess women are here to learn the power and force of ego drive and pride. They have strong, life-affirming energy and determination, which can create a better world if they so choose.

Sun Goddess women thrive on approval and flattery and demand an audience. They also have an attraction to status and appearance, sometimes to the extent of vanity. They sometimes attract insecure or self-doubting partners who are warmed by their Sun energy. Problems can occur, however, if these types of mates become overshadowed by the Sun Goddesses' personalities. Their most suitable mate is a successful and creative soul who has no difficulty in accepting her strengths and is proud of achieving mutual goals.

Before they mature emotionally and spiritually, Sun Goddess women may attract or form partnerships with weak, undeveloped mates who are nothing more than superficial flatterers. In order for them to break this pattern, they must allow themselves to look introspectively into their energy without bias, rather like the sun goddess Amaterasu, who learned to accept her true power when she looked into a mirror. Until they are prepared to acknowledge their part in attracting this type of mate, they may find themselves repeating this pattern of failure over and over.

Sun Goddess women have a naive side to them and sometimes take on the role of the provider and supporter. If they do not balance their masculine drives with their feminine side, they will find themselves reducing the power of their mate's potential to succeed. This will lead to periods of imbalance or an eventual disintegration of the union.

The Sun Goddesses must learn to respect and honor positive power, but at the same time learn to accept input of energy in return. They must learn not to over-nurture their mate. To draw respect from their mates, Sun Goddesses must learn to be more sensitive.

The Sun Goddesses' journey will take them through relationships of unequal power balances, struggle, and disappointment until the necessary growth has been achieved. It is not enough to simply seek the next replacement, they must be prepared to face the truth. They do not suit weaker companions and must have partners who have equally strong egos. Mates should be financially independent and interested in personal development.

Evolving Meditation for Sun Goddess Women

Your vision journey is the power of the sun.

Visualize yourself in a favorite place somewhere out in the open. This may be at the beach, in a forest, outside in a garden, or sitting by a lake or a tree. See yourself sitting peacefully in your place. It is a beautiful, clear, sunny day. You are alone, perfectly safe, there are no distractions, and you are at peace.

Now visualize the sun in the sky shining brilliantly down on you and all around you. Feel its gentle rays warming your body and spirit. (If you have difficulty with visualization, simply place a picture of a pleasant scene in front of you. Make sure you are warm and physically comfortable.) Call to mind any problems or issues troubling you. Then imagine them dissolving like crystals into the warmth of the light as it radiates from within and outside you. While you are visualizing this, accept your inner strength and power as a gift. Realize the great potential you have. If any prior partnerships have failed as a result of insecurities (either yours or your past partner's), perceive them as crystals dissolving in the sun's rays. You are releasing them into the air, setting them all free now.

Then picture the sun as the goddess above you, healing and repairing the energy all around. Breathe comfortably and easily, and with each breath affirm your power and accept yourself. Accept the peace and introspection of your spiritual journey.

Recite to yourself the following:

> "I am evolving in my wisdom and my soul. I have positive and confident people around me. I seek partners who stand in their own power. I allow this to be. I know I will connect with the right energies."

MOON GODDESS RELATIONSHIPS AND KARMA

Moon Goddess women are gentle, feminine, and intuitive. Karmically, they are here to learn inner strength and self-reliance, as well as how to fulfill their creative potential.

Their greatest challenge in relationships is overadapting to their mate's expectations. Often Moon Goddess women have a wonderful capacity to perceive exactly what kind of woman their chosen mate desires and will work at fulfilling this imaginary vision, even when it has very little in common with the person they really are. Over time, however, these women become tired of matching someone else's view of who they should be. They long for an empathetic appreciation of the real self and an equal exchange of energies. Unfortunately, they may have already set the pattern for disappointment by attracting the wrong kind of partner.

Moon Goddess women have all the tools to change this situation. They can develop their intuition and project a stronger and more defined picture of their real personality. In order to do this, of course, they must first discover themselves.

Maturity will bring them much more positive relationships. On the way, however, Moon Goddess women may form intimate bonds with overbearing and emotionally insecure partners who believe they have found the perfect woman to mold and control. They may also attract reasonable but incompatible mates who are merely deceived by their chameleon charms.

Moon Goddess women have such a powerful need of a partner that they will often neglect their talents and skills. They suffer from loneliness and will make sacrifices to keep from being left alone without a mate. Their ideal partner has a sense of humor, is flexible, emotionally secure, and even-tempered. These women endure a great deal of pain from their vulnerabilities and mood swings, so the last thing they need is a temperamental partner.

Moon Goddess women should steer away from mates who are manipulative and have fragile egos or are in any way abusive. Their partners should also have a constant interest in their intimate life or they will become destabilized emotionally. If they cannot find the right mate, they are better off enduring some periods of single life, though this may be very difficult for them to accept.

Evolving Meditation for Moon Goddess Women

Your vision journey is the movement of the moon.

Visualize yourself in a moonlit garden on a balmy summer's night surrounded by flowering roses, jasmine, and daphne. Smell the gently intoxicating fragrances of these flowers. Look upwards to see glittering stars above you against an endless night sky. You can also hear all the sounds of the night: frogs croaking, crickets singing, night birds calling, the soft brushing of leaves swaying against each other in a gentle breeze. (It may be helpful to play a tape of night sounds obtained from the meditation section of your music shop or one that you may have made yourself.)

Focusing your gaze upwards, you can now see the moon. It begins as a slim crescent, then waxes until full and luminous. Relax and listen to your breathing. Breathe in through your nose and gently out through your mouth. Begin to sense your special and unique personality.

Picture yourself sparkling with vitality and energy. If you have any unresolved relationship issues, bring them to mind. Feel the strength you have in your mind and the power in your spirit to achieve your goals.

Then visualize a falling star in the night sky, leaving a trail of light as it moves down along the blackness. Make a wish on it. Then affirm your special energy in the following way:

"I renounce extremes of emotions. I am powerful and unique. I will have a caring and sensitive mate. I face my difficulties. I express who I am. I am centered and whole in myself. I will rejoice in myself."

Practice this simple meditation when stressed or emotionally low.

EARTH GODDESS RELATIONSHIPS AND KARMA

These women are drawn to explore the power of the mother in all her aspects.

Earth Goddess women are often placed in situations during early life where they must care for another. They develop a sense of usefulness from seeing to others' needs and watching the person evolve and mature. Often projecting a warm and genuine interest in people, Earth Goddess women need to learn when to receive in their relationships. They will find themselves in situations that call for them to clearly draw boundaries between themselves and others to achieve a true sense of self.

Earth Goddess women are likely to attract partners who have had a difficult or absent relationship with their own mothers. Sometimes, the partner will be seeking a replacement for something he or she did not have in childhood. This will leave him or her emotionally insecure and seeking condolence.

However, if Earth Goddess women are not careful, they will spend the rest of their life attempting to correct the mistakes of others. They will take on responsibilities that are not their own, and in doing so, inadvertently negate the other person's learning process.

Another problem Earth Goddess women face is overpowering others in the belief they have to have their help. Their focus on life can be too narrow; they see themselves as the *only* people with this power. This will alienate them from many potential friends and partners. In this way also they often neglect to develop their other skills and talents.

Earth Goddess women usually encounter mates that are needy yet noncommittal. They may waste a great deal of their energy attempting to be everything to this person in the mistaken belief that their energy alone can release the mate. They fail to see that each person must be responsible for his or her actions.

Unfortunately, in excess, their energy stifles and restricts. This causes friction, conflict, and loss. Karmically, the Earth Goddesses must learn to respect the divinity of another individual's freedom and energy.

Until they do this, they will continue to encounter unequal relationships. The myth of the Greek goddess Hera, who suffered much unhappiness at the hands of her husband Zeus, illustrates the Earth Goddess's energy in excess. Hera became so obsessed with Zeus's infidelities that she allowed herself to become destructive. She was portrayed as caught in an unequal union from which her only release was to lash out.

Earth Goddess women must realize that they deserve respect and loyalty from their mates. They need to learn to receive respect in all their relationships and to give the same in return. If this does not happen, they should withdraw their energy. This may mean accepting help when offered, and occasionally letting others nurture them instead. It may also mean leaving unequal unions.

Evolving Meditation for Earth Goddess Women

Your vision journey is nature.

Since you relate so much to nature, you need a quiet, natural setting to relax in. Play inspiring and uplifting music by artists like Enya (your Earth Goddess sister).

Relax and breathe easily. Visualize a beautiful open meadow or huge garden and imagine yourself as the gardener. See yourself tending to the plants and trees in your garden. Each plant represents or symbolizes a hope you have at present. This may be in connection with a relationship or other goal. Notice how each of your plants requires different treatment, but not overcaring for. In the same way, meditate on the need for more balance in your emotional and spiritual lives.

Affirm your growth by reciting the following:

"I honor my ability to nurture and sustain. I accept my natural power. I have all I need within myself. I choose to have relationships with mature and caring people. I withdraw my energy where appropriate and respect other's space. I willingly accept respect and nurturing from other people."

WARRIOR GODDESS RELATIONSHIPS AND KARMA

Warrior women are vital and energetic. Karmically, they are here to learn about the power of destruction and creation. Often their karmic path leads them through journeys of conflict and battle with others. This requires them to draw on their reserves of courage and fortitude.

In relationships, Warrior women tend to attract partners who have faced similar conflict in the early part of their lives, but may not have developed sufficient self-reliance. Warrior women will usually extend fight battles for their partners, as this is how they relate to love. They will lose their love, however, in the same way!

The ideal mates for such powerful women are often noble warriors like themselves. They must avoid situations where their strength is taken for granted. As Warrior women portray a bold and capable image, they attract potential mates who may avoid responsibility. This sort of person will want someone else to make all the hard decisions and fight the battles for them.

If they become entangled in these types of liaisons, Warrior women will invariably find that they are eventually discarded when someone else, whom the partner finds more appealing, takes on the battle. Or, having had the battle fought and won (by the Warrior woman), the partner may decide to move on. By becoming caught up in these cycles of give and no return, the Warrior woman ends up being wounded in an emotional battlefield.

Warrior women feel cheated when they do so much for a mate only to be ignored or left. The subsequent disappointment they experience can turn into remorseful anger and resentment. Rather than succumbing to bitterness, Warrior women should realize their energy and its power.

Spending some time researching the tremendous vigor of some of the more ferocious goddesses like Sekhmet and Kali may help the Warrior women realize their true power. In all their relationships, they need to cultivate their gentler and more receptive side. Allowing others to see their vulnerability and accept support in times of strife will help them cultivate wisdom. It may also be important for them to have a transpersonal goal—perhaps helping society in some way or partaking in a charity—to channel their assertive and questing energy constructively.

Evolving Meditation for Warrior Goddess Women

Your vision journey is the "quest for life."

Visualize yourself riding a horse through a field of golden corn. The field stretches out endlessly in front of you, behind you, and at both sides. The sky is a soft pale blue and the wind is blowing through your hair. You feel at peace and centered in yourself. There is no stress and no urgency to do anything. Enjoy your freedom and your relaxation.

As you ride on, you focus on the battles you have fought in the past and the victories you have achieved (this may also include battles in past relationships and conquering them by leaving them behind). Be thankful for each time you have made it through. Congratulate yourself on your power and gift to handle such situations.

Now you are approaching a group of tall, shady trees surrounding a crystal-clear watering hole. You stop to allow your horse to drink and you, too, drink the water. It is cool and refreshing and sunlight sparkles on its ripples as you pass the water in your palm from the pool to your mouth. You are at peace; you are calm and relaxed. Sit there awhile and see around you a beautiful, open field.

Affirm your spirit by saying the following:

"I am the Warrior Goddess. I symbolize victory and merriment. I choose to celebrate my life and share this with others. I choose when to fight and when to play. I invite wise warriors to join me. I acknowledge the power of others to be warriors too, and invite them to join me in my quest."

God Signs & Compatibility

In addition to your Chinese animal sign compatibilities, your Goddess Sign can reveal further fascinating insights into your compatibility with your mate when compared to the equivalent god energy in men (which I have called "God Signs"). The following sections detail men's God Signs and I have linked this energy with their Chinese animal sign. I have illustrated the associations with selected celebrity couples.

For your own personal analysis of male partners, check their animal sign from Table 1 (on page 5), which is the same information for men, and link this to the God Signs below. Remember, the analysis must take into account your karmic learning path as already discussed in the previous chapter.

The following God Signs are characterized with the animal signs as illustrated in Table 3.

Table 3: God Signs and Corresponding Animal Signs

God Sign	Chinese Animal Sign
Sun God	Rooster and Dragon
Moon God	Goat, Dog, and Cat
Dark God	Rat, Monkey, and Snake
Warrior God	Tiger and Horse
Earth God	Ox and Pig

SUN GOD MAN:
THE NATURAL CREATOR

Sun God men are charismatic and energetic with a powerful personality and energy. They are linked to the animal signs of the Rooster and the Dragon. Sun God men are extremely creative and expressive. Unless afflicted, they usually have a quiet dignity and air of control.

Try directing a Sun God man and you may not get a positive response; they love to be top dog. Carried to extremes, this can lead to an overdeveloped ego and relationship difficulties.

They will normally attract many potential mates, but few will really appeal to them as they are perfectionists and rather hard to please. They hold strong ideals and will give generously to subjects. However, they demand loyalty in return.

Immature Sun God men will be status-seeking and superficial with demanding and unreasonable egos. They will also be rigid and dictatorial with violent tendencies if crossed. Mature Sun God men will be warm, affectionate, and loving.

Famous Sun God Men

Russell Crowe (Dragon)

Gregory Peck (Dragon)

Keanu Reeves (Dragon)

John Lennon (Dragon)

Eddie Fisher (Dragon)

George Segal (Rooster)

Steven Spielberg (Rooster)

Michael Caine (Rooster)

David Niven (Rooster)

James Brolin (Dragon)

Associated Gods for the Sun God Man

Apollo: Greek god of the sun linked with art, learning, and culture. The famous temple at Delphi is dedicated to him. Laurel is his sacred plant because it symbolized poetry, with which he was associated.

Zeus: Greek god of supreme power. Zeus was said to have presided over all gods. He was also known as the "Father of Heaven." His mythical home was Mount Olympus.

Ra: Egyptian god of the sun. Ra was the most venerated deity of his time and was said to have begotten all pharaohs.

MOON GOD MAN:
THE NATURAL ARTIST

Moon God men are linked to the animal signs of the Goat, Dog, and the Cat. Intuitive, emotional, and artistic, these men have extremely powerful feelings. At times, these feelings can overwhelm them. Moon God men are prone to very complex relationships in which they attempt to integrate their feminine side with their masculinity.

Moon God men usually develop great passions in life as they can be highly disciplined. However, they are also attracted to escapism and dangerous addictions.

Undeveloped Moon God men are delusional, addictive, paranoid, unfaithful, and escapist. Developed Moon God men are emotionally receptive, nurturing, multifaceted, and humorous.

Famous Moon God Men

John Denver (Goat)

Billy Bob Thornton (Goat)

Mick Jagger (Goat)

Bruce Willis (Goat)

Nicolas Cage (Cat)

Brad Pitt (Cat)

Johnny Depp (Cat)

Geoffrey Rush (Cat)

Sting (Cat)

Bill Clinton (Dog)

George W. Bush (Dog)

Barry Humphries (Dog)

Prince William Windsor (Dog)

Gary Oldman (Dog)

Elvis Presley (Dog)

J. R. R. Tolkien (Cat)

Tobey Maguire (Cat)

Benjamin Bratt (Cat)

Associated Gods for the Moon God Man

Thoth: Divine moon god of ancient Egypt, Thoth was regarded as the source of law, writing, medicine, and magick. He was believed to be the guardian of the mythological gates of the moon.

Anubis: Jackal-headed god of the underworld in ancient Egypt. Anubis guarded the underworld entrance and is associated with the soul's journey from one plane to the next.

DARK GOD MAN:
THE NATURAL MAGUS

Dark God men are linked to the animal signs of the Rat, Monkey, and the Snake. Like their Dark Goddess sisters, they are drawn to the exploration of the underworld in their lives.

Dark God men are highly complex, seductive, and deep thinking. On the surface, many appear conservative, even mundane. The reality can be very different! They often flirt recklessly with danger in a moral, spiritual, and physical sense as if they are seeking to find answers to very profound questions. For this reason, Dark God men have confusion in their lives until they have really matured.

Undeveloped Dark God men are compulsive, obsessional, reckless, and self-destructive. Developed Dark God men are healing, creative, inspiring, and display shamanistic tendencies.

Famous Dark God Men

Sean Penn (Rat)

Prince Charles (Rat)

Bono (Rat)

Antonio Banderas (Rat)

Hugh Grant (Rat)

Ben Affleck (Rat)

Clark Gable (Rat)

John F. Kennedy (Snake)

Abraham Lincoln (Snake)

David Wenham (Snake)

Rudolph W. Guiliani (Monkey)

Guy Ritchie (Monkey)

Michael Douglas (Monkey)

Elijah Wood (Monkey)

Associated Gods for the Dark God Man

Hades: Greek god of the underworld. Hades was the consort of the Greek goddess Persephone. He was also known as Pluto (or Pluton), Lord of Riches as he was believed to know the location of all gems on earth.

Odin: Norse god of death and rebirth. Odin was said to know secrets of mystical knowledge, such as rune magick and sacred poetry.

Ganesha: Hindu god of magick. Ganesha is believed to have begotten Buddha.

WARRIOR GOD MAN:
THE NATURAL WARRIOR

Warrior God men are dominant, leading, and forceful. They are linked to the animal signs of the Tiger and the Horse.

As they may have spent a number of lives defining their purpose, Warrior God men can be very eager to have things their own way in this one! They need to watch impulsiveness, ruthlessness, and fanaticism, as they often see things in black and white. These men have extreme views of right and wrong.

Conversely, Warrior God men can be very powerful in helping others if they turn their energy to humanitarian goals. This is because they have courage and initiative, and others will naturally look to them for leadership. In addition, they often have powerfully magnetic personalities.

Warrior God men will often view their relationships as battlefields until they refine themselves and tame their inner beast. They must be careful of violent passions and compulsions.

Undeveloped Warrior God men are manipulative, demanding, rigid, selfish, and belligerent. Developed Warrior God men are magnetic, charming, empowered, and humane.

Famous Warrior God Men

Tom Cruise (Tiger)   Denzel Washington (Horse)
Bill Murray (Tiger)   Jerry Seinfeld (Horse)
Ralph Fiennes (Tiger)   Kevin Costner (Horse)
Leonardo DiCaprio (Tiger)   Harrison Ford (Horse)
Joaquin Phoenix (Tiger)   Dennis Quaid (Horse)
Matthew Broderick (Tiger)   Paul McCartney (Horse)

Associated Gods for the Warrior God Man

Ares: Greek god of battle and war. Ares was the son of Zeus, the most powerful god in the Greek pantheon.

Thor: The Nordic god of war, Thor was sacred to the Viking people.

Horus: Egyptian warrior god who was said to have killed the god Set as revenge for the murder of his father, Osiris.

EARTH GOD MAN:
THE NATURAL CRAFTSMAN

Earth God men are linked to the animal signs of the Ox and the Pig. Connected to the earth energy, these men need to harness practical and useful talents in themselves to feel fulfilled. They have strong security needs and feel a necessity to be of service to others.

Earth God men are reserved and shy, sometimes needing encouragement to fully express themselves. They need to be careful of inflexibility, negative emotions, and depression. Their strengths, on the other hand, are intensity of purpose and will and the ability to manifest their dreams. They are also capable of very deep feelings and can be loyal and steadfast.

Immature Earth God men are stubborn, dependent, domineering, and unreasonable with fixed ideas. Mature Earth God men are faithful, nurturing, strong, and humane.

Famous Earth God Men

Eddie Murphy (Ox)

Michael J. Fox (Ox)

George Clooney (Ox)

Peter Jackson (Ox)

Jim Carrey (Ox)

Billy Joel (Ox)

Paul Newman (Ox)

Michael Parkinson (Pig)

Rupert Everett (Pig)

Elton John (Pig)

Michael Hutchence (Pig)

Billy Crystal (Pig)

Sonny Bono (Pig)

Fred Astaire (Pig)

Associated Gods for the Earth God Man

Ptah: Egyptian god of handicraft said to have created life from a potter's wheel. Ptah is also regarded as the patron god of builders and craftsmen.

Quetzalcoatl: Aztec god of creation and knowledge. Quetzalcoatl was said to have been the inventor of the Aztec calender.

HOW THE GODDESS SIGNS
RELATE TO THE GOD SIGNS

Sun Goddess Woman and Dark God Man

This can be an electric and fascinating combination, but only if the Dark God man has mastered his struggles. The Sun Goddess expresses warmth, strong ego-drive, and extroversion. This can be a liberating energy for the Dark God man who may have repressed many of his natural feelings during his life.

In turn, the Sun Goddess woman will be drawn to the mystery of the Dark God's drives and his undeniable sexuality. She will be enthralled by his extreme passions and turned on by his profound insights, as she often lives on the surface of life.

On the challenge side, the Sun Goddess will need to be careful of attempting to dominate the Dark God man with her personality and should not overstep the boundaries. The Dark God man will have a strong need for privacy and periods of introspection, which must be respected by his partner. He will not respond well to prying or invasion of his privacy. He may frustrate the Sun Goddess with his mysterious moods. He also has more intuitive understanding than she does, which can throw her.

♡ Celebrity couple:
Catherine Zeta-Jones (Rooster) and Michael Douglas (Monkey)

Sun Goddess Woman and Moon God Man

The Sun Goddess woman, with her strong sense of self, love of power, and shining personality, may attract the Moon God man in a very profound way. He will be drawn to her almost polar-opposite personality and even adapt himself to her energy so they can connect. Over time, however, these two can clash over very different values and ethics.

The Moon God man is sensitive, moody, and subject to changing feelings and perceptions. He has a very complex nature, and the Sun Goddess may feel threatened by his cryptic mixed messages. He may admire her confidence and style, but find her lacking sensitivity and an appreciation of who he really is.

Unless there is great maturity in both parties, this couple may lose their capacity to relate and the partnership will end. Even after it does, many bittersweet memories can remain between them. Where it works, the Sun Goddess can find deep emotional growth.

♡ Celebrity couple:
       (ex) Priscilla Presley (Rooster) and Elvis Presley (Dog)

Sun Goddess Woman and Earth God Man

The Sun Goddess woman and the Earth God man can draw each other through mutual friendship and a sense of nurturing. The Sun Goddess may have gone through a number of superficial affairs and relationships in her life, and will really appreciate the stability of the Earth God man. He, in turn, will be warmed by the Sun Goddess woman's passion for life and her dynamism. The Earth God man's reserve and shyness will at times, however, dampen her natural enthusiasm.

This partnership can work where the Sun Goddess has matured and is able to balance her ego needs with another. In turn, the Earth God man will need to chill out and learn to be open and flexible if he wants this to endure.

♡ Celebrity couple:
       (ex) Renée Zellweger (Rooster) and Jim Carrey (Ox)

Sun Goddess Woman and Sun God Man

This combination is either incredibly successful or a real disaster! The Sun Goddess has an arresting personality that is matched by the Sun God's own perception of himself.

The attraction of these two is assured, but a relationship will depend on tolerance and understanding. Double Sun energy can be creative and magnetic, although there is a risk that both may get tied up in ego battles with each other. If it does succeed, they can be a very inspirational team!

♡ Celebrity couple:
       Yoko Ono (Rooster) and John Lennon (Dragon)

Sun Goddess Woman and Warrior God Man

These two individuals are a complex and formidable unit. He has the courage and drive she admires, but he is not particularly interested in her continual need for attention. His strength turns her on, but not his likely insensitivity. She will push, he will pull, and some very big power struggles can emerge.

This relationship can work where both are prepared to nurture their introspective sides. Although such a development is a lot to ask for from both of them, they can be rewarded by a very enduring connection where each can win.

♡ Celebrity couple:
> Calista Flockhart (Dragon) and Harrison Ford (Horse)

Moon Goddess Woman and Dark God Man

The Moon Goddess woman is a strongly emotional creature who often misunderstands herself. The Dark God man shares her complexity and depth. Together they can often form a bond based on their unique individuality and intuitive sides. Their relationship can be, by turns, passionate, empathetic, and revealing.

As they both have a tendency to go to the dark side of life as it were, they need to be careful of their emotions; they can easily go over the edge of reality. A testing and usually karmic link, there is a great potential for growth here.

♡ Celebrity couple:
> Madonna (Dog) and Guy Ritchie (Monkey)

Moon Goddess Woman and Moon God Man

The Moon Goddess woman finds a soulful connection in the mate of her sign. This partnership usually provides a safe haven from the outside world where both can indulge in shared fantasies and dreams.

They may both have had their share of dubious paramours before they met, and will appreciate the sensitive spirit they find in each other. If they are balanced and mature, a healing, secure feeling will be present.

Both parties must be careful of mood swings and escapist tendencies. The Moon God man may even find he is able to stay faithful to his mate, which is always a challenge for him.

♡ Celebrity couples:
> (ex) Angelina Jolie (Cat) and Billy Bob Thornton (Goat)
> Laura Bush (Dog) and George W. Bush (Dog)

Moon Goddess Woman and Sun God Man

This is a difficult alliance, although at first it can seem to be a fairy-tale union. The Moon Goddess woman plays any role that is necessary to attract her mate and, unless fully mature, is more of an actress than herself in the early stages of courtship. The Sun God man, eager to be applauded and approved of, will delight in his mate's admiration of him. He will see her as alluring and vibrant and will take pride in their connection. As time goes on however, the initial glow may be replaced by uncertainty.

The Moon Goddess must reveal herself at some point, and the Sun God will find a different person exists underneath. Her mood swings will puzzle him, as he dislikes subtlety. She, in turn, may resent his need for space and a career.

This is a rewarding relationship only if both are direct and communicative. It can sometimes work best as a friendship.

♡ Celebrity friends:
    Nicole Kidman (Goat) and Russell Crowe (Dragon)

Moon Goddess Woman and Earth God Man

The Moon Goddess woman and the Earth God man have strong potential for success as he can ground and reassure her. Her delicate sensitivities and need for support brings out his protective instinct, while he also admires her femininity. Provided the Earth God man can learn to express his feelings to his partner, these two can make an enduring and fruitful union together.

The challenges they may face are the Moon Goddess woman's inability to commit emotionally, and the Earth God man's tendency to withdraw when things get too intimate.

♡ Celebrity couple:
    (ex) Cher (Dog) and Sonny Bono (Pig)

Moon Goddess Woman and Warrior Man

This attraction will typically begin quickly and with much electricity. The man in this case loves to feel protective of his mate and will fight battles on her behalf. The Moon Goddess woman will stimulate the Warrior God man's adventurous side and the two will experience true romantic fascination, which may last the test of time.

The success of their union will depend on the value of the communication between them. Neither will express feelings easily as the Moon Goddess woman is reserved and the Warrior man finds it difficult. As a result, confusion and difficulties will often emerge after a period.

His desire to control such a complex mate may meet with repeated resistance that will ultimately frustrate him. She also may feel that he denies her needs for intimacy.

♡ Celebrity couple:
> (ex) Nicole Kidman (Goat) and Tom Cruise (Tiger)

Earth Goddess Woman and Dark God Man

This partnership can be mysterious to both parties, as they tend to intrigue and puzzle each other.

Their initial attraction is based on security. The Dark God man is often seeking stability in his life, needing the nurturing that an Earth Goddess woman could give him. She will feel maternal toward him, and set about providing a retreat to which they can retire. His searching quest for meaning, desire for risk, and dark moods will destabilize her, however, and he will feel smothered by her demands for togetherness.

This can work if one is able to accept the other totally without attempting to change him or her. They must be aware of negative emotions, as these can get out of control with both parties. They also share a tendency to reclusiveness, so periods of too much introspection should be avoided.

♡ Celebrity couple:
> Camilla Parker-Bowles (Pig) and Prince Charles (Rat)

Earth Goddess Woman and Earth God Man

The link between these energies is always empathetic and powerful. The Earth Goddess woman will feel she has truly come home with an Earth God partner who shares so many of her own sympathies.

As long as each partner allows for a free flow of emotion and learns to reveal emotions, this can be a very rewarding connection. It is important that each party allows for spontaneity, however, as there is some risk of stagnation into repeated patterns. Family values and property will form a central focus for these signs.

♡ Celebrity professional partners:
  Ginger Rogers (Pig) and Fred Astaire (Pig)

Earth Goddess Woman and Sun God Man

The Sun God man will feel he has found a valuable ally in his Earth Goddess partner. The main problem here is the Sun God's past. The Earth Goddess will not tolerate fooling around, and the Sun God must move on from his former lifestyle.

He will admire her ability to create stability in his life as he often has a need for organization. She will be immensely proud of his charisma and talents and will do all she can to promote him. She must beware of interfering with his independence, however, as he will not allow it.

♡ Celebrity couple:
  (ex) Meg Ryan (Ox) and Russell Crowe (Dragon)

Earth Goddess Woman and Moon God Man

The warmth and magnetism of the Earth Goddess woman will delight the Moon God. She will understand his delicate sensitivities and allow for his mercurial emotions.

Their main challenges lie in her desire to dominate, and his desire for autonomy and creative growth. She will naturally attempt to heal his wounds, but must be careful she does not overpower him. He may not have the deep sensuality or endurance she requires in a mate, which can lead to sexual difficulties. Both must respect the dignity of the other for this to stand the test of time.

♡ Celebrity couple:
  Hillary Rodham Clinton (Pig) and Bill Clinton (Dog)

Earth Goddess Woman and Warrior God Man

The Warrior God man and the Earth Goddess may respect and admire each other. He may find her strength inspiring, while she respects his drive.

He likes to control and conquer his mate, however, and may not feel challenged by the Earth Goddess. She, in turn, will find some of his power needs confusing, wondering what he is trying to prove.

If both find common interests, this partnership can endure. It may not survive if they lose the ability to empathize with each other, or if the Warrior God man is insensitive to her needs.

♡ Celebrity couple:

> (ex) Meg Ryan (Ox) and Dennis Quaid (Horse)

Dark Goddess Woman and Dark God Man

These two will inevitably share a lot in common. This can either lead to a relationship of deep connection or a clash of very intense wills. Much will depend on what kind of maturity each brings to the partnership.

The ancient Greeks made a ritual of the trip to the underworld called the Eleusinian Mysteries. We do not have an equivalent in our culture, but we live out these journeys in our relationships. The union between two Dark God(dess) people will seem destined and may force both parties to confront the dark side in the other. Both will experience a real jolt of power and far-reaching changes can result.

This union may lead to deep healing or destruction, or a combination of both. The danger of collapsing into the emotions is intensified, however, and needs to be watched by both parties.

♡ Celebrity couple:

> Carole Lombard (Monkey) and Clark Gable (Rat)

Dark Goddess Woman and Moon God Man

This combination of energies has a dreamlike quality. The Moon God man, who is seeking balance with his feminine side, will find the Dark Goddess secure and safe. She has the capacity to close out the outside world and give him time to reach his creativity. He feels drawn to her heightened intuition and magickal perceptions that appeal to his own sense of the world.

The main difficulty in this otherwise positive union will be in the Moon God's inability to commit his emotions to his partner, leading him to experiment outside the relationship. Infidelity and destruction of faith will result, and the Dark Goddess will move away. This can therefore be a complex and sensitive connection.

♡ Celebrity couples:

>   (ex) Jerry Hall (Monkey) and Mick Jagger (Goat)
>   Jennifer Aniston (Monkey) and Brad Pitt (Cat)

Dark Goddess and Earth God Man

The Dark Goddess woman and the Earth God man can make a successful and unique team. Both share a need for security and intimacy. The Earth God man respects the Dark Goddess woman's insights and will honor her. She will be attracted to his constancy and strength.

The challenge side to this union is in each party's need for control. Neither likes to give in, and the Earth God man has a fear of uncertainty. In turn, the Dark Goddess woman will become manipulative if she feels threatened.

For this to work, a mutual understanding on emotional and spiritual levels needs to take place. It will then have the potential to be a productive and beneficial relationship for both.

♡ Celebrity couples:

>   Tracy Pollan (Rat) and Michael J. Fox (Ox)
>   (ex) Kylie Minogue (Monkey) and Michael Hutchence (Pig)
>   (ex) Christie Brinkley (Snake) and Billy Joel (Ox)

Dark Goddess Woman and Sun God Man

The Sun God man is egocentric, proud, and challenging. The Dark Goddess loves to probe under the surface of life, discerning its depths. At first, therefore, these two very different individuals may have little in common. However, a common bond can develop between them.

The Dark Goddess woman can show her mate pathways that he never before considered. In turn, he can provide her with positive acknowledgement, support, and a sense of pride she may never have experienced.

The Sun God's values and external focus can block the real intimacy the union can achieve, however. Also, the Dark Goddess should be aware that she cannot overpower his Sun energy.

♡ Celebrity couples:
> (ex) Debbie Reynolds (Monkey) and Eddie Fisher (Dragon)
> Kate Capshaw (Snake) and Steven Spielberg (Rooster)

Dark Goddess Woman and Warrior God Man

The charisma and innate charm of the Dark Goddess woman thrills the Warrior God man in the early stages of the relationship. He will often try to manipulate her, however, as he does not really understand what makes her tick. She will be flattered by his attentions for a period, but not after he begins to undermine her sense of self-esteem. She will retaliate by using her perceptions and clairvoyance to bring him to heel. These patterns can lead to a union fraught with difficulties.

The main problem lies in very different ways of looking at life. The Dark Goddess needs a great deal of sensitivity in a mate and may not find it here. It can work if the Warrior God develops his gentle side and she restrains her need for control.

♡ Celebrity couples:
> Sarah Jessica Parker (Snake) and Matthew Broderick (Tiger)
> Linda McCartney (Snake) and Paul McCartney (Horse)

Warrior Goddess Woman and Dark God Man

The Warrior Goddess seeks to travel in her mind and body and enjoys mysteries. The Dark God man will entice her with his quest for meaning. He may well be attracted to her strength, vitality, and courage. These lovers may, however, find a lot of difficulty in reaching common ground.

The Warrior Goddess lives her life in a very open and obvious way. She has no use for subterfuge or guessing games. The Dark God man will unnerve her with his need to hold and keep secrets. She will also anger him with her take-charge attitude.

One aspect of this relationship which may well last is the intrigue of it; both will find they cannot fathom the other! Conflicts will often unravel them over time if they cannot learn to communicate real feelings.

♡ Celebrity couples:

> (rumored) Marilyn Monroe (Tiger) and John F. Kennedy (Snake)
>
> Robin Wright Penn (Horse) and Sean Penn (Rat)

Warrior Goddess Woman and Earth God Man

At first glance this association should be a positive one. The Warrior Goddess needs structure and will be grateful for the Earth God man's help in this regard. He will enjoy protecting her brave spirit and assisting her in her busy, hectic life.

The rigidity and soberness of the Earth God man is the main difficulty in this union. She needs and searches for excitement and spontaneity, while he prefers routine. Additionally, he can become angered by her high-handed demands.

♡ Celebrity couple:

> Joanne Woodward (Horse) and Paul Newman (Ox)

Warrior Goddess Woman and Sun God Man

The Warrior Goddess finds herself very powerfully drawn to the Sun God, who expresses so many of her ideals. His charisma and charm work their magick on her, and she will admire his bravery and drive so like her own. Provided both have respect for the other's ego and needs, this can be a really enduring and winning combination.

The difficulties lie in competitiveness and working out who will be boss. Neither is comfortable with backing down in battle! The definition and moral fiber the Warrior Goddess seeks is here however, and she may be wise to work this one out.

♡ Celebrity couple:

> Barbra Streisand (Horse) and James Brolin (Goat)

Warrior Goddess Woman and Moon God Man

These two have a link based on shared humor and drive. She finds his quirkiness and intuition fascinating, while he loves her initiative.

The challenges lie in the famed moodiness of the Moon God man and his changeability. The Warrior Goddess will find it hard to work out his primary motivations. Also, the Moon God man will not sacrifice his natural inclinations for the Warrior Goddess's approval, and much conflict can ensue. The union needs a lot of compromise.

♡ Celebrity couple:
> (ex) Demi Moore (Tiger) and Bruce Willis (Goat)

Warrior Goddess Woman and Warrior God Man

This combination can prove very lasting as long as they stay on the same side.

Compatible as friends as well as lovers, the Warriors make a formidable and resourceful combination. She may have had a number of difficult affairs before they met, sometimes attracting weak or dependent mates. The Warrior God will impress her with his ability to overcome obstacles.

The vital ingredient in this partnership is tolerance and adult behavior in both parties. If this aspect is not present, it can deteriorate into a violent clash of wills.

♡ Celebrity couple:
> (ex) Penélope Cruz (Tiger) and Tom Cruise (Tiger)

Epilogue

In the preceding chapters I have outlined in detail your animal character, your Goddess Sign, and God Sign link. Hopefully this will stimulate you to uncover the greater power of the divine energy within yourself and your fellow creatures. In researching the energy of the Goddess as she manifests in different aspects, we begin to understand the amazing diversity of woman in her scope and features.

If one of modern woman's greatest challenges is adapting to the demands of her life and time, it follows that her greatest strength is to realize her feminine divinity as an asset and an empowerment. The famous women of your particular sign and goddess energy have learned, as if by process of magick, to express their goddess psyche in their work and inspirations and stand as examples for you to follow the enlightenment of the power within.

All signs are diverse—they possess powerful, beautiful, and terrible aspects. This reflects what we are and what we are capable of becoming. This also applies to the divine nature of men.

There is no one manifestation of the Goddess and no typecast for her energies; her divinity is a creative force in us all. From her we learn to value others and ourselves, and realize as women that there is no point in seeking to envy each other on a personal level, as this is to disregard the goddess within.

Greek myth tells us of the legend of the Greek girl Arachne who sought to compete with the goddess Athena. The goddess warned not to disrespect her, but

Arachne could not resist the temptation to weave better than the goddess. Athena punished her by reducing the girl to a spider, spending her life spinning webs all day long. The message is clear: respect the divine power or be reduced to the spinning spider!

As we enter the Aquarian Age, we will go back to the old concepts of the ancient god signs to understand our patterns and purpose, just as the ancient Egyptian and Mayan people did. The goddess power has the capacity to heal society, as does the understanding of our link to our stars and our divine energy. Incorporating knowledge of your divine sign with your relationships will hopefully add a deeper dimension to your life and loves as well as your karmic journeys. May the Goddess embrace and lead us all!

Bibliography

Adams, Jessica. *Astrology for Women*. Sydney: HarperCollins Publishers, 1997.

Adler, Margot. *Drawing Down the Moon*. Rev. ed. New York: Viking, 1986.

Anderson, William, and Clive Hicks. *The Green Man. The Archetype of Our Oneness with the Earth*. San Francisco: HarperSanFrancisco, 1991.

Andrews, Ted. *Animal Speak*. St. Paul, MN: Llewellyn Publications, 1993.

———. *Dream Alchemy*. St. Paul, MN: Llewellyn Publications, 1991.

———. *How to Meet and Work with Spirit Guides*. St. Paul, MN: Llewellyn Publications, 1992.

———. *Magical Dance*. St. Paul, MN: Llewellyn Publications, 1992.

Brandon, Ruth. *The Spiritualists*. New York: Alfred A. Knopf, Inc., 1983.

Brooke, Elisabeth. *A Woman's Book of Herbs*. London: The Women's Press, 1992.

Buckland, Raymond. *Buckland's Complete Book of Witchcraft*. St. Paul, MN: Llewellyn Publications, 1987.

Budge, E. A. Wallis. *Egyptian Magic*. New York: Dover Publications, 1971.

———. *The Gods of the Egyptians*. 2 vols. New York: Dover Publications, 1969.

Cabot, Laurie. *The Power of the Witch.* New York: Delta Books, 1989.

Caddy, Eileen. *Footprints on the Path.* Findhorn, Scotland: Findhorn Press, 1991.

Campanelli, Pauline. *Ancient Ways: Reclaiming Pagan Traditions.* St. Paul, MN: Llewellyn Publications, 1991.

———. *Circles, Groves and Sanctuaries.* St. Paul, MN: Llewellyn Publications, 1992.

Campbell, Joseph. *The Masks of God: Primitive Mythology.* New York: Viking Press, 1959.

Cheiro. *Cheiro's When Were You Born?* London: Herbert Jenkins, 1931.

Chetwynd, Tom. *A Dictionary of Symbols.* London: Thorsons, 1982.

Cicero, Chic, and Sandra Tabatha Cicero. *Creating Magical Tools.* St. Paul, MN: Llewellyn Publications, 1999.

Conway, D. J. *Animal Magick: The Art of Recognizing and Working with Familiars.* St. Paul, MN: Llewellyn Publications, 1995.

Cunningham, Scott. *The Complete Book of Incense, Oils & Brews.* St. Paul, MN: Llewellyn Publications, 1989.

———. *Cunningham's Encyclopedia of Crystal, Gem and Metal Magic.* St. Paul, MN: Llewellyn Publications, 1995.

———. *Magical Herbalism.* St. Paul, MN: Llewellyn Publications, 1987.

———. *The Truth About Witchcraft Today.* St. Paul, MN: Llewellyn Publications, 1988.

———. *Wicca: A Guide for the Solitary Practitioner.* St. Paul, MN: Llewellyn Publications, 1988.

Cunningham, Scott, and David Harrington. *The Magical Household: Spells & Rituals for the Home.* St. Paul, MN: Llewellyn Publications, 1987.

Davidson, H. R. E. *Myths and Symbols in Pagan Europe.* Syracuse, NY: The University of Syracuse Press, 1988.

Davis, Wade. *The Serpent and the Rainbow.* New York: Simon and Schuster, 1985.

Denning, Melita, and Osborne Phillips. *Practical Guide to Astral Projection.* St. Paul, MN: Llewellyn Publications, 1987.

Downing, Christine. *The Goddess: Mythological Images of the Feminine.* New York: Crossword Publishing Co., 1984.

Driver, Tom F. *The Magic of Ritual.* San Francisco: HarperSanFrancisco, 1991.

Drury, Neville. *Pan's Daughter.* Sydney: Collins, 1988.

Elliot, Roger. *Who Were You?* London: Granada, 1981.

Farrar, Janet, and Stewart Farrar. *The Witches' Goddess.* Custer, WA: Phoenix Publishing Inc., 1987.

Forty, Jo. *Mythology: A Visual Encyclopedia.* London: PRC Publishing, 1999.

Fowles, John. *The Magus.* London: Pan, 1966.

Frazer, Sir James G. *The New Golden Bough.* New York: Criterion Books, 1959.

Gaddon, Elinor. *The Once and Future Goddess.* San Francisco: HarperSanFrancisco, 1989.

Glisic, Helen. *Spellbound: Book of Love.* Sydney: Random House, 1998.

González-Wippler, Migene. *The Complete Book of Spells, Ceremonies & Magic.* St. Paul, MN: Llewellyn Publications, 1988.

Graves, Robert. *The White Goddess.* New York: Farrar, Straus and Giroux, 1966.

Jung, Carl G. *Man and His Symbols.* London: Aldus Books, 1964.

Justason, Barbara. *Astrological Sex Signs.* New York: Arco Publishing, 1984.

K, Amber. *True Magick: A Beginner's Guide.* St. Paul, MN: Llewellyn Publications, 1990.

Kempton-Smith, Debbi. *Secrets from a Stargazer's Notebook.* New York: Bantam Books, 1984.

Lyle, Jane. *Tarot.* London: Hamlyn, 1990.

Shimano, Jimmei. *Oriental Fortune Telling.* Tokyo: Charles Tuttle and Co., 1981.

Sommesous, Nicole. *Magickal Book.* London: Thorsons, 1999.

Tyl, Noel. *Astrology of the Famed.* St. Paul, MN: Llewellyn Publications, 1996.

Indexes

GODDESSES

People

Free Magazine

Read unique articles by Llewellyn authors, recommendations by experts, and information on new releases. To receive a **free** copy of Llewellyn's consumer magazine, *New Worlds of Mind & Spirit,* simply call 1-877-NEW-WRLD or visit our website at www.llewellyn.com and click on *New Worlds.*

☽ LLEWELLYN ORDERING INFORMATION

Order Online:
Visit our website at www.llewellyn.com, select your books, and order them on our secure server.

Order by Phone:
- Call toll-free within the U.S. at 1-877-NEW-WRLD (1-877-639-9753). Call toll-free within Canada at 1-866-NEW-WRLD (1-866-639-9753)
- We accept VISA, MasterCard, and American Express

Order by Mail:
Send the full price of your order (MN residents add 7% sales tax) in U.S. funds, plus postage & handling to:

Llewellyn Worldwide
P.O. Box 64383, Dept. 0-7387-0294-3
St. Paul, MN 55164-0383, U.S.A.

Postage & Handling:
Standard (U.S., Mexico, & Canada). If your order is:
Up to $25.00, add $3.50
$25.01 - $48.99, add $4.00
$49.00 and over, FREE STANDARD SHIPPING
(Continental U.S. orders ship UPS. AK, HI, PR, & P.O. Boxes ship USPS 1st class. Mex. & Can. ship PMB.)

International Orders:
Surface Mail: For orders of $20.00 or less, add $5 plus $1 per item ordered. For orders of $20.01 and over, add $6 plus $1 per item ordered.

Air Mail:
Books: Postage & Handling is equal to the total retail price of all books in the order.
Non-book items: Add $5 for each item.

Orders are processed within 2 business days. Please allow for normal shipping time.
Postage and handling rates subject to change.

SignMates

Understanding the Games People Play

BERNIE ASHMAN

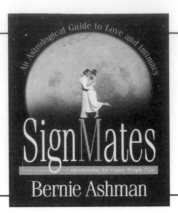

It is mystery and intrigue that leads many of us to play the relationship game, regardless of how our Sun signs are supposed to get along. *SignMates* dispels the myth that only certain Sun signs are compatible with each other. Any two signs can learn to establish a reliable stability. This book will show you how.

The "game" is defined as a repetitive pattern of negative behavior that interferes with the harmony of a partnership. It is an imbalance of energies, often of a subconscious nature. Take for example, the "Missing the Boat" game played by Aries and Gemini. It begins when these two fast-paced signs continuously frustrate one another's actions and ideas. Aries' desire to follow immediate impulses clashes with the Gemini instinct to think before leaping. The challenge is to acknowledge one another's needs and potentials. By working through the strategies suggested for your sign combination, you can turn your differences into assets rather than liabilities. These pages will help you to better navigate your romantic encounters and create more effective ways to communicate.

1-56718-046-9
504 pp., 7½ x 9⅛, 17 illus. $19.95

Invoke the Goddess
Visualizations of Hindu, Greek & Egyptian Deities

KALA TROBE

Appeal to the Hindu goddess Sarasvati to help you ace an exam. Find your ideal long-term partner through Isis. Invoke Artemis for strength and confidence in athletics.

Invoke the Goddess shows you how to link with the specific archetypal energies of fifteen different goddesses through simple exercises and visualizations. This magickal workbook allows anyone, no matter how limited or developed her occult prowess, into a direct encounter with a powerful archetypal deity whose symbols and presence will make a profound impression on the subconscious.

Whether you want to accomplish a specific goal or integrate the murkier areas of your psyche, this book will lead you step by step through your inner journeys. The author explains different ways of carrying out the exercises, how to take ritual baths with solarized water, and preparation through chakra work, diet, and exercise.

1-56718-431-6
240 pp., 7½ x 9⅛, illus. $14.95

Teen Goddess
*How to Look, Love, & Live
Like a Goddess*

CATHERINE WISHART

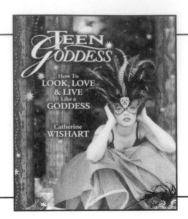

Every girl is a goddess! When you access your goddess power, you can make your life exactly as you want it to be. This positive and hip guide to beauty and spirituality will show you how—with simple messages and tasks that will illuminate your mind, body, and soul.

Remarkable things will happen when you begin to delve into your divine beauty and listen to the inner voice of the Goddess. Find romance, ace exams, radiate confidence, and enchant everybody with your appearance and your attitude. All the glamour, strength, and magic that was available to the ancient goddesses is available to you now.

0-7387-0392-3
408 pp., 7½ x 9⅛, illus. $14.95

The Goddess Path
Myths, Invocations & Rituals

PATRICIA MONAGHAN

For some, finding the goddess is a private intellectual search, where they can speculate on her meaning in culture and myth. For others, she is an emotional construct, a way of understanding the varying voices of the emerging self. Then there are those for whom she is part of everyday ritual, honored in meditation and prayer. All are on the goddess path.

If you have never encountered the goddess outside your own heart, this book will introduce you to some of her manifestations. If you have long been on this path, it will provide prayers and rituals to stimulate your celebrations. *The Goddess Path* offers a creative approach to worship, one in which you can develop and ritualize your own distinctive connection to her many manifestations from around the world.

1-56718-467-7
288 pp., 7½ x 9⅛, illus. $14.95

Book of Hours
Prayers to the Goddess

GALEN GILLOTTE

Here is a book that moves beyond the conscious mind and into the heart and spirit. It is not about theory, techniques of ritual, or even of "practice." It is, simply, a book of goddess-centered prayers, meditations, and affirmations. It includes morning, evening, and nightly prayers; seasonal prayers (for the Wiccan holy days); and prayers for the new and full moons.

Prayer is, essentially, speaking with Deity, but many people are confused about how to do this. This book will unveil the confusion. It is written for young and old, for the neophyte as well as the accomplished Priest or Priestess. It may be used in Wiccan circles, study groups, or anytime you want to connect to the Goddess. Ultimately, it is for those who have a deep hunger for that spiritual connection.

1-56718-273-9
144 pp, 5¾₁₆ x 8, hardcover $14.95

To order, call 1-877-NEW-WRLD
Prices subject to change without notice

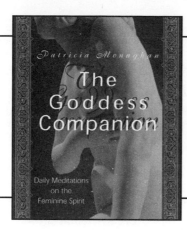

Goddess Companion
*Daily Meditations
on the Feminine Spirit*

PATRICIA MONAGHAN

Engage your feminine spirit! Here are hundreds of authentic goddess prayers, invocations, chants, and songs—one for each day of the year. They come from dozens of sources, ranging from the great classical European authors Ovid and Horace, to the marvelously passionate Hindu poets Ramprasad and Ramakrishna, to the anonymous gifted poets who first composed the folksongs of Lithuania, West Africa, and Alaska. In fresh, contemporary language that maintains the spirit of the originals, these prayers can be used for personal meditation, for private or public ritual, or for your own creative inspiration. They capture the depth of feeling, the philosophical complexity, and the ecological awareness of goddess cultures the world over.

Organized as a daily meditation book, *Goddess Companion* is also indexed by culture, goddess, and subject, so you can easily find prayers for specific purposes. Following each prayer is a thoughtfully written piece of prose by Patricia Monaghan which illustrates the aspects of the Goddess working in our everyday lives.

1-56718-463-4
408 pp., 7½ x 9⅛ $17.95

To order, call 1-877-NEW-WRLD

TO WRITE TO THE AUTHOR

If you wish to contact the author or would like more information about this book, please write to the author in care of Llewellyn Worldwide and we will forward your request. Both the author and publisher appreciate hearing from you and learning of your enjoyment of this book and how it has helped you. Llewellyn Worldwide cannot guarantee that every letter written to the author can be answered, but all will be forwarded. Please write to:

Angelica Danton
℅ Llewellyn Worldwide
P.O. Box 64383, Dept. 0-7387-0469-5
St. Paul, MN 55164-0383, U.S.A.

Please enclose a self-addressed stamped envelope for reply,
or $1.00 to cover costs. If outside U.S.A., enclose
international postal reply coupon.

Many of Llewellyn's authors have websites with additional information and resources. For more information, please visit our website at:
http://www.llewellyn.com